# GALLIPOLI

Arthur Beecroft in his army uniform, *c.* 1915

# GALLIPOLI
## A SOLDIER'S STORY

*ARTHUR BEECROFT*

*Foreword by*
ANDREW ROBERTS

ROBERT HALE · LONDON

ISBN 978-0-7198-1654-3


Robert Hale Limited
Clerkenwell House
Clerkenwell Green
London EC1R 0HT

www.halebooks.com

A catalogue record for this book is available from the British
Library


2  4  6  8  10  9  7  5  3  1

Printed in Great Britain by TJ International Ltd

Those heroes that shed their blood and lost their lives ... you are now lying in the soil of a friendly country. Therefore, rest in peace. There is no difference between the Johnnies and the Mehmets to us, where they lie side by side here in this country of ours ... You, the mothers who sent their sons from far-away countries, wipe away your tears. Your sons are now lying in our bosom and are in peace. After having lost their lives on this land they have become our sons as well.

*Kemal Ataturk, founder of the Turkish Republic,*
*speech extract, Anzac Day 1934*

# CONTENTS

*Frontispiece: Arthur Beecroft in army uniform* (c. 1915)

Map of Suvla Bay area (August 1915)   8

Foreword by Andrew Roberts   9

Preface   13

Introduction: The Reason Why   17


**GALLIPOLI: A SOLDIER'S STORY**

*An Apology*   23

1. Training   25

2. With the Division   45

3. To an Unknown Destination   53

4. Final Preparations   69

5. The Landing at Suvla Bay   79

6. The Dawn   89

7. The Eighth of August   105

8. On Snipers   125

9. The Ninth and Tenth   129

10. Out of the Line   137

*Afterword: Some Psychological Aspects of War*   143

Endnotes                                            151
Timeline of Key Events of the Gallipoli Campaign    154
Major Players                                       157
Glossary                                            171
Bibliography                                        175

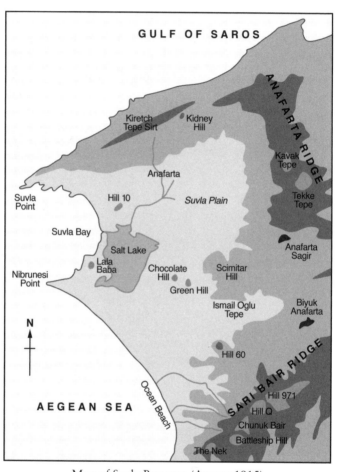

Map of Suvla Bay area (August 1915)

# FOREWORD
## BY ANDREW ROBERTS

'No plan survives first contact with the enemy,' said the great Prussian strategist Helmuth von Moltke the Elder, and this was never more true than of the Gallipoli campaign of the Great War. By April 1915, when the campaign was launched, hundreds of thousands of Allied soldiers had been killed in the trenches of the Western Front, which stretched from the English Channel coast all the way to the Swiss border. To attack the Dardanelles and thereby force the Ottoman Empire out of the war seemed like a brilliant masterstroke – and so it might have been were it not for the dogged resistance of the Turkish army to the assaults launched that month on Cape Helles and Anzac Cove by the Allied expeditionary force.

The attacks were ambitious – dawn amphibious assaults on a relatively unknown coast, with new troops going into action for the first time – and, as it turned out, they were over-ambitious. Trenches were dug at Gallipoli and the soldiers were condemned to the same static trench warfare being endured by their comrades in France and Flanders.

In August 1915 General Sir Ian Hamilton's Mediterranean Expeditionary Force made one last effort to break the total deadlock that had set in on the Gallipoli peninsula. An important aspect of the operation was the landing of most of the newly arrived IX Corps in Suvla Bay, with the intention that they would quickly overrun a lightly held area and assist the Australians and New

Zealanders (Anzacs) as they attempted to break out of their tight little bridgehead around Anzac Cove.

Compared to the titanic struggle on the Western Front, there is a marked lack of memoirs of frontline fighters in the Gallipoli campaign of 1915–16, and still fewer from the Suvla Bay aspect of that campaign. We are, therefore, very fortunate to have a vivid account by Arthur Beecroft, a 1914 volunteer signals officer in the Royal Engineers, attached to Brigadier-General William Sitwell's 34th Brigade, in Major-General Frederick Hammersley's 11th (Northern) Division. The 10th, 11th and 13th Divisions – all new formations of Kitchener volunteers – made up Sir Frederick Stopford's IX Corps embarking on its first ever active service in very trying circumstances. Beecroft wrote his account for his young son.

Arthur Beecroft's earnest intent is to rescue his comrades-in-arms from subsequent accounts of the operation that heap blame upon the Suvla Bay divisions for the dismal failure of the whole August offensive, with the implication that they were 'just not up to the job'. Australian writers have been particularly scathing about the British at Suvla, but Beecroft mounts a vigorous defence of these 'civilian soldiers' and makes important observations on three aspects of their service: their training, their state of health, and their leadership.

Their training in England was, of course, in preparation for the trench warfare in France and Flanders. Beecroft describes it as thorough and 'pretty severe'. These young soldiers embraced the army life with enthusiasm: 'Our troops, despite their embryo training, were determined to make good'. What they were not ready for, just as the troops landing on 25 April 1915 were not ready for, was a full-scale amphibious assault against a defended coast. There simply was no doctrine for such a thing in 1915. Having been told by many historians that these troops could make no preparation for the landings apart from getting in and out of the boats, Beecroft adds very valuable information by telling us that his brigade made two practice landings before the real thing, with a particular emphasis on getting signals communications to follow the attacking infantry. Sadly, they made a complete hash of it on both occasions, merely reinforcing the lesson that amphibious assaults are particularly difficult and night operations even more so.

Beecroft, from his position attached to brigade headquarters, is able to comment on all the most important aspects of the operation. He reminds us that, in the final analysis, military operations are carried out by human beings who suffer from fatigue, thirst and the stress caused more by a fear of letting their comrades down than of the enemy and the battle itself. The troops landing on Suvla Bay on 6 August 1915 had slept little in the lead up to the attack. They were not used to the fierce heat of a Turkish summer and would drink the available water too quickly and be plagued thereafter by thirst. To keep the operation as secret as possible from the enemy, the attacking units were given no advance warning of the assault and all were hopelessly uncertain of what was expected of them, especially when the boats began landing in the wrong places and out of sequence.

Most importantly, these young Northerners rapidly fell victim to Eastern Mediterranean diseases. In a telling passage, Beecroft asks to what extent future historians would take account of the way food could not be conveyed from plate to mouth without becoming covered in glistening fat flies newly arrived from the open latrines used by men wracked with dysentery and diarrhoea. Beecroft reckoned that fifty per cent of the men in action on 6 – 9 August 1915 should have been on a medical sick list but were too keen to see action to report to their unit Medical Officer. Many of these problems could have been alleviated by a vigorous and determined leadership. Suvla Bay should be infamous for the extraordinary degree of failure in the higher levels of command. Sir Ian Hamilton had specifically requested that young, experienced generals be sent out from France to carry out this difficult operation, but he was flatly refused until after it was too late.

Beecroft hints at failures at the level of corps, division and brigade. General Stopford was appointed by seniority but had never commanded fighting troops in action in his long career. General Hammersley, as everyone knew, had suffered a severe nervous breakdown at Aldershot in 1911 and had to be physically restrained in a mental asylum. Writing to his chief, one of Ian Hamilton's officers would later say, 'I thought it was a wicked thing ever to have sent him out there'. Beecroft often mentions 'My General', meaning William Sitwell, and his incapacity to grasp the wonders of the telephone. This 'dug out' general 'had never been equal to such a strain'. As the battle plan unravelled, Sitwell looked 'old and haggard, worn out with worry and physical exhaustion'. Beecroft was in a good position to see how brigade headquarters, despite its responsible Brigade Major and younger staff officers, simply ceased to function as a directing body with such a commander. There is no sense of blame attached to these men so completely out of their depth; rather the blame rested with the authorities in London who expected Hamilton to achieve great things with the barest minimum of resources.

Beecroft ends by making many interesting observations on military psychology and on writers who opine on the terror of battle. Unlike them, he remembers fondly how 'the thin line fought on with true Northern fortitude'. Their failure was 'only a reflection on the training of Kitchener's army, not its spirit'. In this centenary year, the discovery and release of such an important new memoir is a major publishing event, providing a significant increase in our knowledge of a generally under-appreciated part of the Great War.

*Andrew Roberts*
www.andrew-roberts.net

# PREFACE

Arthur Beecroft was my grandfather. *Gallipoli: A Soldier's Story* is his account of an epic struggle which, however heroic, ended in failure. In telling his young son, Bobby, the story of the landing and fighting at Suvla Bay in the summer of 1915, he was passing on the values and code of behaviour that he and his generation of Britons lived by.

What the pages of his previously unpublished manuscript revealed to me is that my grandfather had a strong sense of duty, a Kiplingesque sense of devotion to King and Country, a love of fair play and a deep-rooted sympathy for the underdog. His reaction to Germany's invasion of neutral Belgium was to respond, along with thousands upon thousands of his fellow Britons, to Lord Kitchener's appeal for volunteers in August 1914.

In his eagerness to get to the fighting in France, Arthur bought himself a motorbike and joined the army as a despatch rider. With his public school and university background (Tonbridge, The Leys and Cambridge), it was not long before he was offered a commission in the Royal Engineers. He took it up readily because it seemed to hold the promise of a quicker way to France. The decision-makers in London, however, had other ideas. The war in France had reached a stalemate, with a steady drain on lives to gain a few yards of ground. To Winston Churchill and those who shared his views on matters of strategy it seemed that taking Gallipoli would shorten the war by threatening Constantinople and forcing Turkey to sue for peace. Gallipoli, then, was the destination of Arthur and thousands like him.

At school and in the army he had learned how to give orders and how to take them. At Suvla he gave praise where praise was due – which was not very often – but his memoir criticizes orders that he had to obey even if he believed them to be unnecessary and potentially wasteful of lives. What he tends not to do is to name names. Reticence, even in cases of stupidity, was part of the unwritten code. And so, throughout his memoir, rather than spell out names of individuals, Arthur would use the literary convention of an initial letter followed by a long dash.

I found his manuscript in the loft of my parents' house after their deaths. It was typed on yellowed paper between the covers of a plain blue folder. It had lain undisturbed for over half a century. I sat down and read his story until I had reached the end. I was surprised that this period in my grandfather's life had never been mentioned in any family discussion, even though he had been awarded the MBE in 1922. It was his service in the Home Guard in World War II that was the more general topic when we were growing up after that war.

My grandfather was a colourful character in many ways. As a young man he travelled across the United States in a stagecoach and also explored parts of South America. After losing an eye from infection, he would often wear a monocle, which made him quite scary to us grandchildren! He was highly principled and expected one to do one's best at all times; he sometimes had a short temper and didn't suffer fools gladly. He was a fearsome adversary as a barrister in Court. Between cases he would sit at his typewriter in his chambers and write detective novels and plays. After the First World War he published three books under the pen-name of Arthur Salcroft: *The Mystery of the Walled Garden* (1928); *The Twisted Grin* (1929) *and John Traile: Smuggler* (1929). From his days at university he loved sport and was a rugby blue. He was a passionate gardener and later in life he loved to paint rural scenes in and around Buckinghamshire where he lived most of his life. He died in a nursing home in Gerrards Cross in 1974.

Special thanks to my good friend Robin Hosie for writing the background material presented in boxes throughout this book and so providing a context for my grandfather's memoir.

*Prue Sutton*

# INTRODUCTION:
# THE REASON WHY

'The main essential to success in battle is to close with the enemy, cost what it may.... During the delivery of the assault the men will cheer, bugles will be sounded and pipes played.'

*Infantry Training Manual*, 1914

The Gallipoli campaign was one of the most audacious Allied gambles of the First World War. If it had succeeded it could have shortened the war, but through a combination of poor planning, incompetent generalship, stout resistance by the Turks, and sheer bad luck, the campaign ended in failure for the Allies. Its legacy was humiliation for Great Britain, a stain on the reputations of many in high places, and a memory of extraordinary heroism that ended all too often in pointless sacrifice.

No military enterprise is ever without risk, but at the beginning Gallipoli seemed to be a risk worth taking. Great Britain declared war on 4 August 1914 following the German invasion of Belgium. At the time, it was a guiding principle of British foreign policy that no great power should be allowed to occupy the Low Countries because an invasion fleet assembled there would be, in effect, a dagger aimed at Britain's heart. This clashed with an equally strong guiding principle in Berlin: that a war on two fronts was to be avoided whatever the cost. Germany's Schlieffen Plan called for a massive right hook that would knock out France, leaving the victorious German army to turn its full might against Russia.

Britain's small Regular Army, sent across the Channel to help the French, was at first able to do little but retreat in fighting order. 'A contemptible little army' was how Kaiser Wilhelm II dismissed the Tommies. This was a rash statement by a rash man, for by mid-September the German advance had been fought to a halt. Both sides dug in and a zigzag line of trenches began to appear, stretching from the North Sea to the Swiss frontier. What had been expected to be a war of rapid movement and short duration turned into a slow desolation of slaughter. By day and by night the ordeal imposed by machine-gun and rifle fire, mines and shrapnel-packed, high-explosive shells was made even more unbearable by mud, rats, lice and barbed wire.

To the fertile mind of Winston Churchill, then First Lord of the Admiralty, there had to be a way to break the stalemate. Germany might be the world's most formidable land power but Great Britain was by far its greatest sea power. Could the whale bring down the elephant, as it had done over one hundred years before, when Nelson at sea thwarted the ambitions of Napoleon on land? Churchill's gaze turned towards the Dardanelles. If Allied warships could force a way through this narrow 45-mile stretch of water and threaten Constantinople (modern Istanbul), then Turkey might sue for peace, a route could be established for sending war supplies to beleaguered Russia, and Germany might be forced to divert troops from the only place where the war could be won or lost – the Western Front.

Lord Kitchener, Great Britain's War Minister, reluctantly agreed to the strategy, but only because he was given assurances that Allied ships could force a way through on their own, and there would be no need to divert manpower from the trenches in Flanders. A fleet of elderly British and French battleships was assembled. Now all they had to do was to run the gauntlet of the Dardanelles.

*Robin Hosie*

A folio of the original manuscript, with contemporary
photographs of Arthur Beecroft

# GALLIPOLI
## A SOLDIER'S STORY

# AN APOLOGY

I have written some detective novels since the War, but until recently had no intention of writing a war book. Just lately, however, you, Bobby, to whom I am dedicating this MSS, have shown an interest in your father's doings in the Great War, and it suddenly occurred to me that you might read some of the war literature of the times, thus perhaps being led to misjudge not only the millions of men and women who laboured for the Empire for five weary years, but also your own father.

You will soon discover in reading this MSS that I was neither hero nor particularly good soldier; and that my war experiences, though out of the ordinary, were not thrilling. My story, however, is the same kind of story which countless ex-servicemen could tell, and it is a far truer reflection of the war than most of the books which have obtained a large circulation of recent times. This MSS will never be published for many reasons, the chief one being that the public are getting sick of the subject – and a good job too!

I wonder how future historians will tell the tale of 1914–1918. Will they stress the wonderful efforts of the Empire? Or will our children's children hear of nothing except disarmament, The League of Nations, and the

Kellogg Pact?[1] Will my grandchildren be told that I was a civilian who tried (with somewhat indifferent success) to become a soldier for genuinely patriotic motives, or shall I be represented as a poor bemused fool who was led blindfold to the slaughter, and who had not the gumption to see that his ideals were sham?

I have one other good reason for putting my war experiences into writing, for I am told that I am one of the few now surviving who took part in the landing at Suvla Bay in August 1915, and I have recently seen the official history in the making at the War Office. I now wish to get down my own account before age colours the imagination.

# 1

## TRAINING

I was in the Isle of Wight when war was declared. The friends who were with me all hurried home, most of them with some definite idea of getting into the army without delay.

I was terribly torn as to my duty. My father was no pacifist, but he had always hated anything to do with military affairs. His own grandfather had fought in the Napoleonic Wars in the Navy and as a midshipman had received his baptism of fire at the early age of thirteen. From then on until he was thirty he was constantly fighting, and he was demobilized (or rather axed!) as a captain when he was but thirty-one, with numberless battle-scars to mark his services. My father was brought up on his war stories, and of the brutality of fighting. No wonder that he would not let me join the Cadet Corps at school, for he only saw the one side of war, just in the same light as our present historians are writing of the Great War. Perhaps you, Bobby, will get so fed up with my stories that you will take drastic steps over the education of *your* son!

Arthur Beecroft (*second from left; standing*) with members of
the varsity tennis team, Christ's College, Cambridge, *c.* 1907

The position was, therefore, that by the 4th August
1914 I had never received the slightest training, and had
never fired anything but a shotgun in my life. Into the
bargain I had one very weak eye, which not only was
likely to give trouble under bad conditions but would
probably prevent me from getting a commission.

I went home to Tunbridge Wells, and hung about
there in the greatest misery of mind. It was vacation
time, so that there was no work at the Bar to keep me
occupied. I tried to play golf, or raced around in the
family car, my greatest excitement being the latest war
edition of the newspapers.

At that time the majority of people believed it would
be a short war. Personally I believed that six months

26

would see it through. I thought that our Expedition-ary Force would be sufficient to turn the scale, and I regarded the actions of those of my friends who joined up as mere gestures of patriotism. That they would ever actually fight seemed incredible in August 1914. They could surely never be turned into real soldiers, and by the time they had been trained the war would be over.

I was very annoyed when I was asked by a member of the golf club when I was going to join up. His origin was German, too! The poor old man had a thin time later in the war, but I really believe he was entirely British in sympathies.

Then came the German drive through Belgium, and the sudden realization that our own army was actually on the retreat. I shall never forget the day when I read of the German successes. I was sitting in the car in our garage, gazing at the huge headlines of the paper, which seemed to dance before my eyes:

## FALL OF NAMUR

So the Germans were advancing through Belgium as easily as a farmer's boy would stride through his mas-ter's hay. The new, wonderful Belgian forts had simply collapsed under some terrible modern guns.

Paris next? What could stop them? I had been brought up with a pretty healthy contempt for the French, for had not we given them a good hiding a century ago, while the Germans had smashed them up in a brief campaign in 1870?[1]

My mind turned to our small Expeditionary Force. I got a sudden longing to be with it. It would feel so

---

# The First 100,000

In what was to become the world's most famous poster, a piercing-eyed, sternly mustachioed Lord Kitchener points an accusing finger and delivers the message: 'Your Country needs YOU.' In the early days of World War I, as a field-grey tide of German troops swept through Belgium, he was looking initially for 100,000 volunteers to augment Britain's superbly professional but dangerously small Regular Army.

He got them within two weeks. Recruiting offices were swamped by up to 33,000 volunteers a day. They came from the shires and the suburbs, from department stores and factory floors, from stately homes and back streets. One of their most powerful motivations was pride in an Empire on which, it was held, the sun never set. For Arthur Beecroft, the subaltern at Suvla, and for thousands of others, the last straw was the violation of Belgian neutrality.

---

much nicer to take one's chance in the field rather than to live to acknowledge the Germans as conquerors. It was an incredible thought that the Germans might beat us. Even the Channel might not prevent them invading England and marching on London! I fancied the Empire broken up, the Kaiser in Buckingham Palace.

I suddenly slipped off to Cambridge, where the authorities were recruiting officers. I put in an application, and my worst fears were realized: my eyesight was hopeless.

A few days later I decided to join the University and Public Schools Brigade, familiarly known as the UPS. Getting into it meant two days hard 'queuing', and a little deceit over the eyesight test, but I was for the present an entirely happy man.

It was extraordinary what relief of mind was gained by joining up. It was nothing to do with any external pressure. I never saw any girls with white feathers and, except for the well-meaning gentleman at the golf club, I was never pressed to enlist. Yet I knew that I must be in it, and I was utterly miserable until I was. If ever there is another war, Bobby, most Englishmen will feel the same way, in spite of any amount of disarmament, pacifism and the like. And the itch to be doing is not bred of heroism or anything like it, but merely the old idea of comradeship. If you know that your forebears have fought for your country, and that your own friends and neighbours have gone, you have simply got to go, too, or brand yourself, not necessarily a coward, but a non-sport who doesn't play the game: like the fellow who can't stick rough play at rugger and gets 'crocked' as an excuse or a boxer who takes the 'count' as an easy way of dodging punishment – they are hallmarked, and so was I until I had joined up.

There are few books which will tell you of the enthusiasm of those early days in 1914, or, if they do, will give you an adequate idea of the joy of service which most men felt. I remember marching with the battalion down Oxford Street – over a thousand public school and varsity men – singing our early war songs. Every window was crammed with cheering people, and the streets were lined. Can't you guess how we strutted and thrust our chests out? Childish though it may have been, dreadful harbinger of miseries to come, we all felt the exaltation of the moment, and we shall never forget it. When you hear some of the old marching songs sung by ex-servicemen, you'll see their eyes go misty and their bodies straighten up. They are not thinking of the horror of war, but are transported to the glamorous days when 'being with the boys' brought its own exaltation.

The original idea of the UPS was that we should be trained and serve as a special battalion of public-school men, our NCOs being selected from our own number. Although this was carried out later, the early stages of training were made very difficult through numerous recruits being withdrawn at once for commissions, and also by defections for various reasons. At first there were insufficient trained soldiers to act as instructors, so that we could only be taught the rudiments of infantry drill, the rest of the time being occupied by route marches. At this early stage I was not in the least mindful of the dangers or horror of war, but I did find that my fortitude was badly shaken by route marches! I have always loathed walking anyway, and always as I trudged along in the battalion dust with the perspiration pouring off me, and my blistered feet protesting at every stride, my mind would turn to thoughts of horses, motor-cars, or even push bikes!

We were sent into camp at Epsom. I had joined up in the same company with a number of school friends, but our happy band soon became separated. Some received commissions, others were given the red ribbon of non-commissioned rank. C— W— and I were left together and I soon found that he also had other ideas for the future.

I remember one awful morning when the battalion was sent out on a route march. We were still in

## The King's Commission

Officers in both the Regular Army and Kitchener's New Armies were chosen almost entirely from the privileged classes. Those seeking His Majesty's commission to lead troops in battle needed to be well enough off to pay for their own uniforms and were generally expected to be gentlemen by birth as well as by temperament. They had to be smart, alert, versed in military law and used to leadership. The right to buy a commission had been abolished as recently as 1870, but underlying social attitudes do not always change in step with the law. In the first few months of the Great War, education at a grammar school rather than a public school was an effective bar to many young men applying for a commission.

Britain's class system, however, was never a rigid caste system. A handful of officers in the old Regular Army had been promoted from the ranks. And a fair number of young men in the New Army, although they had the 'correct' public school and university credentials, joined up in the first place as private soldiers. Arthur Beecroft, the subaltern at Suvla, was one of them.

our 'civvies', and our thin boots were giving out. We plodded along for twenty-five miles of macadam roads, and then the men started dropping out. I remember that we completed the last mile in a series of halts and trots, my mind registering hate for foot-slogging to the exclusion of any other thought.

It was, I believe, the next day that C— W— made his suggestion. We had a friend who was recruiting motor-cycle despatch riders for immediate service in France. We could probably obtain a transfer to the Royal

Engineers, when we should receive the rank of corporal, special pay – and no more foot-slogging! I have always thought that I rather shirked the onerous life of the PBI, but in extenuation I can say that in October 1914 the despatch riders (or DRs, as they were called) were rather looked upon as members of a suicide club, so that our decision was not skrimshanking.

*– i –*

## The Sappers

I purchased a Triumph motorcycle in Holborn and rode it down to Chatham to report for duty. I there obtained my first insight into the Regular Army.

I feel somehow that this history is going to cut across many popular ideas. Even in 1914 I expected to find supercilious officers, brutal NCOs, and absurd red tape. I got my early shock in the QM's stores.

'Well, young man,' said the QMS, 'so you're coming into the corps straight away as a corporal.'

It occurred to me that the regulars would surely be very irritated to see a number of civilians suddenly put up two stripes and take their place in the NCO's mess. In normal times it required long service and much hard work to get such promotion, yet here we were without the slightest military knowledge, our only asset being the ability to drive a motorbike.

I filled up the necessary particulars under the eye of the NCO.

'You're a college man,' he nodded. 'Just wait until I

have dished out these stores, and we'll go over to the mess.'

I found a number of NCOs there, and I was shown around and given a drink. In spite of the fact that our special enlistment as corporals was very unpopular, all the NCOs were quite pleasant. C— W— and I were 'college' men, and they regarded us as curiosities who might be forgiven.

I took the greatest pride in my new corps, and this early introduction to the regular sappers was of the nature of an eye-opener. The buildings and huge parade-ground were impressive, while the smartness of the men and NCOs filled me with awe. Would I ever be able to get my puttees to look like those of the QMS? We passed an officer, and his correct acknowledgement of the salute made me want to thank him!

We had arrived on a Saturday, and there was nothing doing on the following day. I suggested leave, at which the QMS said that we might just ''Op it, only mind you are back by nine o'clock Monday morning.' Actually we did not arrive until eleven, but did not receive any more severe reprimand than the acid comment that we were 'fair knock-outs'!

Our Depot was to be Aldershot, and we rode our machines down there on the following day. I do not know what Aldershot was like in peacetime, but it was pretty fair hell in 1914. There were about five times more troops than the barracks could accommodate, with the consequence that we had to go under canvas. This is no hardship when the weather is suitable, and one is in the country, but a very different matter in a barrack square when there is no sort of supervision.

On arrival at the QM stores I was given a tent and some blankets, and told to get busy. A few other arrivals soon joined us and proceeded to get properly entangled with pegs and guy ropes. An old soldier finally put us wise. We found that twenty-one other recruits and reservists were also interested in that tent.

C— W— and I knew nothing of army proceedings. When rations were served out we came off very badly, and we decided to go down to the town for our meals. We found a small eating house, but the rough food tasted fine. That night we all got into that tent somehow, but as some were exceedingly drunk I did not get much sleep.

The following day was rather worse. The quick enlistment of recruits had disorganized machinery which was only expected to deal with a small depot, and the nerves of officers and NCOs were frayed with overwork and worry. At my first parade I got properly ticked off for being unshaven, and my excuse that there was nowhere to wash made things worse. We could never get our share of rations and I lost my new blankets. In my cheerful ignorance I asked the QM for another issue, and retired a wiser and saddened man, a concise description of my application following my hasty exit. Thus did I learn the necessity for 'scrounging', and I had three blankets again that night, of which two were new ones!

Matters in the tent were not improved when it was discovered that I was a corporal. Most of my tent companions were reservists and they were openly contemptuous of our two stripes – 'for just driving a bl**** motorbike'. Someone had to be in charge of the tent, and as I had enrolled before C— W—, I was senior. It took my mind back to schooldays, to my first duty as a sub-prefect in a dormitory full of small boys who were out to test new authority. However, I was determined not to give in, and I secured some sort of unwilling obedience.

The Engineers' Depot was composed of a number of different companies according to training. We motorcyclists were about 150 strong, with Captain C— and two subalterns in charge. Captain C— was a most excellent soldier, except that he was so anxious to get to France that his heart was only half in the Depot work. We must have been a queer lot to train. The nature of the DRS had attracted a mixed crowd of racing motorists, young varsity men, and harum-scarums. We were immediately taught the rudiments of map-reading and signalling generally, including schemes for carrying messages under war conditions. Never did I see such wild riding, and the peremptory orders of Headquarters, with punishment for offenders, could not stop it. It certainly was a temptation to drive fast, with perfect roads, no interference from the police, and wartime enthusiasm. We always had DRs in hospital all over the countryside. There was a great thrill in tearing through some peaceful town with perhaps fifty others, although the residents must have got very sick of it.

Casualties amongst the DRs in France were high, so that drafts were being constantly requested. As soon as a draft was formed, leave was stopped, special equipment issued, and one's motorcycle tuned up. There was also the inoculation – a beastly business which usually laid you out with a high temperature for about forty-eight hours.

'On draft!' Exciting thought! Soon were to come flying

journeys under shellfire, over roads torn to pieces, where a mistake in map-reading might land you in the German lines. We would handle our clumsy revolvers and wonder whether we could shoot straight from the saddle! I may add from later experience that, judging from the average display of revolver practice on the range, I doubt whether the ordinary DR would hit a house! Our imaginations coloured the work of the DR on service, for in fact the roads were so bad that steadiness was required rather than speed. The work was dangerous, calling for coolness and care rather than any heroic qualities.

My draft was due away on a Saturday. On the Friday beforehand I was ordered to report to the general commanding the Royal Engineers. I had no idea what was in the wind, but duly reported. On being admitted to the general's presence I found him examining some report.

'Sergeant Beecroft?' he asked, looking up at me closely.

'Sir!'

'Your name has been sent in for a commission.'

'I know nothing of it, sir. I have not applied.'

'That may be; but it has been suggested that you would do well as an officer.'

I thought of the draft; of C— W— and my other friends who would go abroad without me; and though the idea of a commission sounded rather pleasant I shrank from it.

'How would you like a commission in the infantry?' the general was asking.

More foot-slogging! No!

'What branch of the service would you like?'

I knew the sappers had been very chary of taking

on temporary officers, so that if I specified that corps I would probably be turned down and go with the draft.

'I would only take a commission in the REs, sir,' I replied firmly, and expected to be told off. The general, however, was rather pleased. He asked me innumerable questions about myself and my past, and then, to my great surprise, intimated that he would recommend me for a commission in the corps.

And so I said goodbye to the draft, and to C— W— and my other pals. I felt as if I had kept out of service abroad rather unworthily, and that they thought so too. Even now I have regrets, for I would like to have been able to say that I served as a DR in France. As it was to be, I was never to serve in France at all.

## – ii –

I departed from the DR company, and was posted to a young officers' course. This was supposed to take six weeks and included the general training for signals, in which we had to learn flag-wagging, Morse, telegraph and telephone, and gained some superficial knowledge of the instruments. I was often out of my depth, especially with some of the more complicated apparatus.

It was rather humorous that I had got myself out of the infantry by means of a motorcycle, and now found that I had to learn to ride a horse. If I needed punishment I certainly got it. The riding course was the most drastic affair. I can still see that riding school with the ring of horses, and the NCO with his whip in the centre of the ring.

'Cross your stirrups!'

One would jolt round the ring, precariously poised on the slippery saddle, gradually losing balance, desperately catching at the saddle when the sergeant wasn't looking.

'Let go 'o your saddle, there!'

And crack would go the whip, the horse would jump playfully, and off I would go!

It was absolute agony, with one's legs almost paralysed and perspiration pouring down one's face. And there was no mercy whatever. Every day for weeks we were driven round that school or out on Laffan's Plain, until at last some sort of seat was acquired.

Into the bargain there was the training with the cable wagon. This was drawn by four horses, the drums of telephone cable being fixed on the rear, to be paid out as the wagon proceeded. A mounted man followed with a crook-stick, hitching up the cable along hedges and out of danger.

The trained horses were wonderful. You could take a toss right in the middle of a galloping ring of horses, yet never be kicked. The beasts never required any control by the individual rider (which was just as well), and would obey the order of the riding instructor instantly. The cable horses were simply astonishing, for they knew the job as well as the trained soldiers. If, for instance, the cable suddenly came off the drum with a rush, the horse would slacken up to give the man with the crook-stick time to deal with the coils. Then, with the line becoming taut, your horse would gallop off. Sometimes the crook-stick would get entangled, so that if you hung on to it you might get dragged off; but your horse would know instantly, pulling up dead to give you a chance to free the stick. All this would be done without any control, for many of us had little idea how to manage a horse at all. Those animals were like circus horses, and they simply loved their work.

I was never good with horseflesh, for I had started too late in life. I could ride fairly well after a time, but I was never happy as a horseman and took some bad tosses, especially when I was given a couple of brutes which were only half broken. I also disliked stables, especially of the early-morning variety.

It is to me a curious fact that writers about the war continually harp on about the same causes of a soldier's discontent of mind: of fear of death, dirt, disease and physical exhaustion; but I really believe that I was more worried by my inability to cope with my horses than ever I was by anything else. I knew my weakness, and could not conquer it.

The course was not unlike a university training. One had classes every day, with periodical examinations, and a test of efficiency which had to be passed. Much of the work was done at the Signal School, the remembrance of which is always associated in my mind with military funerals, for the cemetery was close to it, and casualties through disease, especially amongst the Highlanders, were very heavy, so that our buzzers were often drowned by the wail of the bagpipes.

With other young officers I was accommodated at a supernumerary mess at Vine Cottage. We dined at the officers' mess proper in the Stanhope Lines. There, we met mostly regular officers, and were kept well in our proper place. There was occasionally trouble when some young officer committed a breach of etiquette, but we were very well received on the whole, and I enjoyed myself enormously. It would generally be the more senior regular subalterns who caused trouble with 'temporary' officers, and seldom the seniors, although one or two crotchety majors rather delighted in jumping on us. I count myself very fortunate to have seen something of our pre-war Regular Army, and to have served with its officers and men. As a result I found my respect for it grow every day of my training, and I know now that our civilian armies would never have been so good as they turned out to be if it had not been for the tremendous efficiency of that small Regular Army.

I passed most of the tests fairly comfortably, except for the riding certificate. This was quite severe, consisting of rough riding over Laffan's Plain before the CRE. I managed to stick on until we came to the final charge up to where the general was seated in state, but lost my irons, reins, and nearly everything else which keeps the rider attached to his mount. There was no reason why my horse should stop at all, except that he was thoroughly well trained, but when he had duly planted his for feet firmly down in front of the general, I of necessity proceeded somewhat further, and nothing but the fact that my horse had a pair of large, well-planted ears saved me from falling at the astonished general's feet. In passing out the class, the latter had a few private words for me, from which I gathered that I had had a close squeak from being sent back to the riding school.

## – *iii* –

When nearly at the end of my instructional course, I was suddenly called to see the Depot commandant. I found that my late OC of the DR company had gone off with a draft of DRs, taking with him his subaltern and senior NCO; that the War Office had demanded yet another draft of some eighty DRs, and there was no one to see to its preparations.

I was told to do my best. There were only about eighteen hours in which to find the men and machines, and I knew nothing whatever about the company, as I had not been concerned with it since receiving my commission. I rushed off down to the company offices, to find but one NCO available to help me.

'You are going to have the devil of a time, sir,' he remarked genially. 'The whole company has just been inoculated and most of 'em can't move.'

'What about the machines?' I asked. 'Are they ready for service overseas?'

This he did not know, and the mechanics seemed to have gone off to help with the last draft. I did have the devil of a time. We had to try every machine ourselves, and then find who was ready for instant service. I now only have a dim memory of working all night in the yard examining machines and holding parades of men who could only stand with difficulty. They clearly could not ride to Southampton, so I was soon engaged with arrangements for a special train, and for lorries to get the draft to the station. The commandant could not give much active help, but he stood by with encouragement.

We got down to Southampton with a full comple-
ment of men, but lost a machine somewhere en route
– probably it was never put on the train. I comman-
deered another in Southampton, and my last job was to
get the men from the station to the docks. Of all the
proceedings, this was quite the worst. The poor devils
were at the worst stage of inoculation. They were sick
and dizzy, while some of them had high temperatures.
I never heard a grouse, but I felt pretty bad at ordering
them to ride their machines. They did it somehow, the fit
men doing two journeys to fetch their pals. There were
spills, but no serious accidents, and with great relief I
saw them on the transport, complete.

The commandant did not throw a bouquet at me,
but a week later I was posted to take command of the
DR company. I had about 150 DRs on the strength,
about 200 machines with large workshops, and a couple
of cars for my own use. It was some job for a subaltern of two month's service, and the best I had in the
war. Regular NCOs stood by me and the commandant
was always ready with his support, not only then, but
throughout the war. I shall never forget him: quiet in
manner, and with few words; steely eyes which missed
nothing; the finest type of RE officer, which is saying
quite a lot.

For two months I trained DRs. We roared around
the countryside, learned all about maps and the organ-
ization of the army; fired revolver courses (with much
danger to surrounding buildings, the birds and myself),
and absorbed a little discipline. They were a great crowd
in those early days, drawn from all classes, and all full
of keenness.

In early spring I asked the commandant to send me abroad. I was soon posted to the XI Division, encamped at Witley, then preparing to go abroad for immediate service.

# The War Horses

It was an unquestioned item of military wisdom in 1914 that cavalry would play a key part in the battles to come. Its traditional role was to turn the flanks of an opposing force, to sweep behind enemy lines, gather information, exploit breakthroughs, disrupt communications and spread panic. It was calculated that Kitchener's New Armies would need 245,000 horses, but Britain had nowhere near enough to meet the demand. Horses and mules had to be brought in their thousands from as far away as Australia and America.

In these memoirs, Arthur Beecroft recalls how close he came to despondency because of his poor horsemanship. He need not have worried. Trench warfare put a swift and brutal end to the romantic idea of the dashing cavalry charge. Apart from a few small and indecisive actions, cavalrymen were used, both in France and in Gallipoli, as no more than dismounted infantry. Horses and mules were still needed for bringing up supplies and hauling heavy guns into position, and these poor dumb creatures had to face the same risks and terrors as their masters. It was Winston Churchill, brought back into the government as Minister of Munitions in 1917, who saw the problem most clearly. He questioned the wisdom of keeping 30,000–40,000 men in the cavalry and suggested they could be better used in tanks and armoured cars.

# 2

## WITH THE DIVISION

It was quite a drop to go from a large company, in which I had exercised an independent command, to a divisional signal company in which I was one of the most junior officers. In the first place I knew little of the technical side of signals, for my course had been cut short and I had had no practice since I had taken over the DR company. I also knew very little of the internal working of a signal company, and still less of Brigade signals to which I was immediately posted.

My division was one of the early Kitchener enlistments, and a finer bunch of men I never met. Mostly North Country they were, and their training had been pretty severe.

My general was a 'dug out', and I never got on with him. He always looked upon me as a mere civilian in uniform and was slightly contemptuous of signals anyway. I gathered at our first interview that he had been told by the Command Staff that his 'signals' were hopeless, and gathered that I was expected to put everything right at once.

## Turning Civilians into Soldiers

The rush of volunteers responding to Kitchener's appeal over-whelmed the country's capacity to train them. In the first few months of the war there were not nearly enough barracks, uniforms, weapons or instructors to go round. The men and boys of Kitchener's New Army might find themselves billeted in church halls, schools, warehouses, or even private homes. Those without uniforms had to sew regimental patches on to their civilian clothes. Some early recruits marched on to the parade ground wearing red jackets left over from the Boer Wars. Rifles were in such short supply that in places men had to slope arms using broom handles. Arthur Beecroft, hoping to get to France as a despatch rider, had to buy his own motorbike. The Order of the Day seemed to be 'Make Do and Muddle Through'. For some volunteers the training pro-gramme was compressed into as little as six weeks, and they arrived in France not even knowing how to fix bayonets. But order began to emerge out of chaos. Slowly but unstoppably, a mighty army was being forged.

It was amazing how some of the old retired army officers, whose service had, probably, only been in the Boer War, simply could not understand the importance of their signalling sections. The general said frankly that he knew nothing about the subject. He had been used to the telegraph for distance work, or to helio; with runners or flag-wagging for shorter communications. He hated the telephone, and I constantly had to show him how to use the ordinary portable, the betting being two to one that he would speak into the wrong end.[1] I soon found that my RE section was not well trained, while the battalions always detailed their worst officers and men for battalion signals. It was depressing in the extreme, my only relief being the support of the brigade major. He was my sheet anchor, and he stood between me and the general's foolishness. In fact, as hereafter appears, he subsequently undoubtedly saved my life.

While at Witley Camp I tried to train my section and to get their confidence. It was almost a case of the blind leading the blind so far as the technical side was concerned, for the reasons I have already given, but gradually I got to know my job better. My CO at Divisional Signals was too busy with the HQRS Company to spare much time for my section, so I was thrown back on my own resources.

In looking back at my section I find that I have two quite separate ideas of each one of them. There is first my opinion of NCO or man under training conditions at Witley, and then the revised edition after each had fought at Suvla Bay. You can never tell how any man will shape up to real fighting.

There was my driver, X, a small sulky youth who was always getting into the hands of the civilian police for being drunk and disorderly. First I admonished him in paternal style; then I gave him the usual CB; and finally took him before my CO. It all had no effect. Then one day I found that he was sick with the toothache, lying in his tent with an abscess like a cricket ball in his cheek. I took him straight off to the dentist, and saw to it that he got proper attention afterwards. There was no more trouble with Driver X. Just because he had been given the same attention as one would give a sick animal he was a different man. He had found someone who displayed an interest in him other than in his crimes. I can still see Driver X with his mules, trudging along the shore at Suvla: dirty, sullen, but getting on with his job.

I had great trouble with a man I will call Sapper Y. A barrack-room lawyer he was, and a damned nuisance. It was the greatest difficulty to persuade him to clean himself, and he loathed shaving. 'Y' would appear on parade with his chin covered with black stubble.

'Why haven't you shaved this morning, Y?'

'I have shaved, sir. I think my army razor is a dud, sir.'

I felt as if he watched me, grinning at my scanty knowledge, and hoping I would trip up on some point in the King's Regulations. He was liable at any moment to quote KR, and I have no doubt that he studied them assiduously. You will hear more about Sapper Y later.

In those early days of training I had far too much to worry over in my own work to think much about the division. Physically the men were simply magnificent, and from my vantage point at the head of the brigade on route marches I used to look back over the swinging column of finely proportioned men, with the certain feeling that so far as material was concerned there could be no doubt about the calibre of Kitchener's Armies. A cheerful crowd they were, too, and my section gave them a good lead with a mouth-organ band.

Route marches were anathema to me, for I led the brigade column, being responsible for the route. I was mounted, and I believe that no officer in the British Army could have been given worse horses. I had three of them. One was a beast which I only mounted once.

It then reared and fell on me, so I handed it over to the rough-riding sergeant for his opinion. The animal went over on him three times in ten minutes, and I refused to have anything more to do with it. The next was a brute with a scar extending from eye to muzzle. A half-broken Argentine horse he was, and he must have been treated with great cruelty, for whenever anyone approached from either side he would instantly shy away, and would get into a lather of fear. You can imagine what it was like riding such a horse: when it was constantly necessary to take messages, or to ride up to the general; while the brute would often see someone on the side and jump right across the road. A third horse I had, with a trot that made my teeth chatter, and a mouth like iron. He was as slow as a hearse, but he was quite capable of running away with me, and I never discovered any method of stopping him. You will laugh and say I couldn't ride, which is perfectly true, but if I had been given a decent horse there would have been no difficulty about it.

Even now I can hear the general roar: 'Keep the bloody horse still, man!' And I would be trying to hand over some service message to the old man, while my cursed horse, as soon as he saw the general stretch out his hand, would edge a little further away.

I saw some awful brutes at different times which had been sent from the Remounts. I wondered who selected them. It may be rather fun for a good horseman to master a spirited animal, but it was no sort of game to have to carry out technical mounted duties as officer or man while mounted on a brute of a horse with all my time taken up trying to manage him. I suppose that, as a mere brigade signal officer, I was given the worst of the horses, and perhaps what were supposed to be (although actually they were not) the least satisfactory men; just in the same way as battalions, in the early days, detailed their least-wanted officers and men for battalion signals. This seems as if I have a big grouse; and I have, for you will hear what sort of job signals were given at the landing at Suvla Bay.

I got on very well with battalion staff officers, and in a very short time the COs gave me more willing help. History will relate that the senior officers of the division were drawn mostly from the reserve; that they were no longer young; and that they were lacking in both up-to-date training and energy. The younger staff officers, on the contrary, were most excellent, although their efforts were often hampered by the slow uptake of their superiors. As it turned out, we needed encouragement as well as drive. We should have got both if the younger regular officers had been in command.

We had no regular mess during training, for the staff officers generally were in outside quarters with their wives. Until we embarked for the East I had little social intercourse with anyone, but what few social relations I had were quite pleasant. I was always called 'Flags' by the general, and sometimes I was referred to as 'the civvy', for I was, I believe, the only civilian soldier on the brigade staff. The general was very keen on chess, and I was easy prey. We would sometimes discuss the mundane affairs of the world outside the army, and then I used to feel rather lonely.

Then we received orders that our destination was the East. Helmets were issued, and we busied ourselves with buying tropical kit. Meanwhile everyone was asking about our destination. Was it to be Salonika? Or the Dardanelles? All enquiries were met with a mysterious lack of information.

# Disaster at Sea

It was an error — the first of many in the Gallipoli campaign — for the Royal Navy to engage in minor action near the entrance to the Dardanelles in the closing months of 1914, for this put the Turks on the alert. Liman von Sanders, the German general appointed to modernize the armed forces of the Ottoman Turks, was not a man to ignore such a free gift. With Prussian efficiency he built up Turkish defences on Gallipoli and on both shores of the Dardanelles. When the expected naval attack came on 18 March 1915, and sixteen Allied battleships steamed into the straits, Turkish forts and Turkish guns were ready for them. Worse still, the Dardanelles had been sown with a deadly crop of mines. There were minesweepers, largely crewed by civilians, with the Allied fleet. But so narrow are the straits – in places hardly more than three-quarters of a mile across – and so heavy was the Turkish fire, that the minesweepers had to turn away before completing their work. One minefield had been laid with such skill that it lay undetected – until it worked. Three Allied battleships were sunk in the narrows and others suffered heavy damage. The fleet retired to lick its wounds. Only later was it discovered that the Turkish guns were running out of ammunition and their resistance was on the point of crumbling. There was bravery to excess in the attempt to force the Dardanelles by sea, but the 'warships alone' plan was misconceived.

# 3

## TO AN UNKNOWN DESTINATION

The journey out East calls for little comment. We had a comfortable ship, excellent quarters and food, and it would have been a joyride except for the danger of submarines.

We stopped at Malta and Alexandria. With a party I went on a night prowl in Alex.; and if I wanted to bring in the sex stuff which is featured in most war books, I could do it right here. I will only say, however, that we visited a number of brothels, high-class, low-class, and disgusting; that in not one of them could we get a drink because of the military regulations (a pretty good test of the far-reaching effect of British authority); and that in our wanderings only one of our party of about sixteen fell by the way. In parenthesis I will add that, as a result of my experience during the years when I was adjutant of a Depot through which tens of thousands of men and at least a thousand officers passed, I do not believe in these highly-coloured tales of drink and women. I do not mean that there was not drunkenness – most of us had our 'binges' – nor that there was not quite a lot of

# The Army Takes Over

After the costly failure of the attempt by an Allied fleet to force its way through the Dardanelles Straits, the entire Gallipoli project might have been abandoned. But Lord Kitchener was persuaded to swallow his doubts and give grudging approval to a plan to take the peninsula by land. He allocated some 70,000 men to this operation and put in command General Ian Standish Monteith Hamilton, who had been his Chief of Staff in the Boer War. Once Hamilton's troops had driven the Turks from the dominating central plateau of Kilid Bar, the guns protecting the straits could be silenced. Then the way would be clear for an Allied fleet to reach Constantinople and to dictate terms. So, at least, went the theory.

Hamilton set up headquarters on the Greek Island of Lemnos and worked out a two-pronged strategy. The British 29th Division was to storm ashore on five beaches at Cape Helles, on the tip of the peninsula, and some 15,000 men of the Australian and New Zealand Army Corps (ANZAC) were to strike about a dozen miles further north, in an area that was to become famous in history as Anzac Cove. These landings would be supported by two diversionary attacks – one at the neck of the peninsula, the other by a French colonial division at the mouth of the Dardanelles on the Asiatic shore.

In an address to his troops Hamilton announced: 'We are about to land on an open beach in face of positions which have been vaunted by our enemies as impregnable … the positions will be stormed and the war brought one step nearer to a glorious close.' The reality was tragically different. Hamilton, who was equipped with inadequate artillery, had no true knowledge of the strength of the opposition, and did not even have up-to-date maps of the peninsula. He brought

> no sense of urgency to the task and did not launch his attack
> until 25 April – a full five weeks after the naval failure. Mean-
> while, the Turks, urged on by their dynamic German military
> adviser, Liman von Sanders, used this breathing space to
> triple their forces on Gallipoli from two divisions to six.

immorality; but considering the loosening of restraint, and wartime temptation, I think that the British soldier kept a marvellously tight hold of himself. When one did hit upon someone lascivious or drunken, he usually got little encouragement. And this applied, mind you, in a Depot to which officers addicted to drink were deliberately sent. I don't believe the sappers would have allowed any officer to remain on active service if he could not keep going except by booze. Furthermore, the average officer was far too scared of disease to rush off for promiscuous intercourse with any woman.

My son! Read the real histories of the war if you wish to study it from the military side; and beware of the book which makes a dirty story out of it. As you grow up you'll have your own temptations to face in civilian life, and you'll meet the type who will tell you that all men are vile, and most of the women, too. That may be a comforting belief for a man who wishes for plenty of company in his degeneracy, but it is neither true of present days, nor of the war time.

We went first to Mudros, where we had our first taste of Eastern conditions. It was hot during the day, and cold at night, and I was seriously disturbed by the

# Attackers

Brigadier-General Sir Aylmer Hunter-Weston, commander of the 29th Division, had some peculiar ideas about how to inspire his troops on the eve of battle. 'Expect heavy losses by bullets, by shells, by mines and by drowning,' he warned them as they readied themselves to storm Cape Helles. Encouraged or not by such words, the 29th hit five beaches on the tip of Gallipoli, at dawn on 25 April 1915. The Turks could not give adequate cover to every possible landing-place, with the result that three of the landings met little opposition. The other two beaches became death-traps. The Lancashire Fusiliers, Dublin Fusiliers, Munster Fusiliers and Hampshires attacking W Beach and V Beach were given a vicious foretaste of what was to come. The Lancashires won six VCs that day.

V Beach was overlooked by cliffs with an old fort on the crest, and was defended by riflemen and machine- gunners who were well dug in. The attackers ran into a hailstorm of bullets and many died before their feet could touch dry land. The sea at V Beach turned crimson, with more than half of the 950 men in the first wave killed or wounded. Nevertheless, the survivors managed to drive the Turks out of their trenches and to establish a beachhead. On W Beach, a 200-yard strip of sand overlooked by cliffs in front and on both sides, a single company of Turks – some 200 men – caught the attackers in a murderous crossfire from rifles and machine-guns. Eventually, the Turks were driven from their trenches, but while Hunter-Weston, aboard ship off W Beach, showed little inclination to press ahead, Liman von Sanders was making sure that Turkish reinforcements were on their way.

The first objective of the Helles landings was to capture the high ground of Achi Baba, key to the strategically vital

Kilid Bahr plateau. After three ferocious battles near the village of Krithia, Achi Baba remained in Turkish hands. The invasion never got further than a few miles inland, and in July Hunter-Weston was sent home with what was officially described as 'sunstroke'. Less sympathetic observers put it down to nervous collapse.

unsuitability of my gabardine uniform which had been recommended for service in the East. One became wet through with perspiration so that the stuff clung clammily to the flesh, and then the chill of the night air struck to one's very marrow. Here also we were introduced to flies – clouds of them. They were not so easily scared as the English variety, so that they were not to be brushed from one's face or food. It was a constant fight with them, and a losing battle at that. We all acquired a feeling of desperation as we vainly tried to protect our eyes, necks and each mouthful of food. They bit one hard, too, so that faces and hands became spotted with blood. I guess we were all sweet – at any rate for a time! There was a French hospital at Mudros, and the conditions there were appalling, but nothing horrified me so much as to see the sick and wounded vainly trying to beat off the flies. In writing the history of the calamities of Gallipoli there will be numerous theories to account for failure, but I wonder whether anyone will put our troubles down to the flies? I do not think there can be any doubt that most of the disease was spread by them, and I guess I know why I personally spent four years as a crock with all kinds of internal troubles ending with 'itis'.

Imbros was our final base before operations. It was a bleak spot with little to recommend it, already occupied by Australian and other troops. My first impressions included the spectacle of an Australian sentry who presented arms to me, and who then saw a full-blown general in whom he was so interested that he completely forgot to salute at all. We marched to our camping ground, where I saw a huge crater formed by an aerial bomb. I gazed up into the clear sky and realized that real war had now commenced.

The first night under canvas provided some fun. I had managed to wangle my camp bed through the baggage, a luxury almost unknown in the division. I soon had a message from the divisional staff – would I care to give it up to some bigwig general who hadn't got one. I went to the brigade major for advice. He grinned at me: 'I'm blowed if I would give it up after having the sweat of getting it through,' he replied.

So I refused, and heard no more about it. That bed felt extra comfortable that night! Having read some of the German books, I wonder what would have happened if a junior subaltern in the German Army had refused to give up his bed to a general!

While waiting for orders at Imbros we continued our training, but it was very half-hearted. We were all keyed up for some expedition, of which we had no information but which we guessed was to be of a pretty desperate nature. The original landing at Cape Helles had been, as everyone already knew, one of the most bloody shows of the war, with an underlying hint of mismanagement about it. Doubt had already been thrown on the soundness of the attack on the

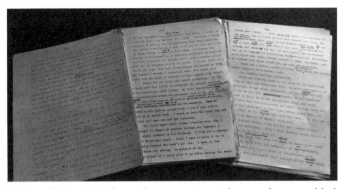

Folios of the original typed manuscript with amendments added
later in hand by Arthur Beecroft

Dardanelles in the first place, and in the back of my
mind was the uncomfortable feeling that we were about
to make a last desperate attempt to break through in
spite of the fact that some of the best regular troops
had failed to do it. In that waiting time at Imbros there
was no despondency, but the atmosphere was tense,
and the talk grim.

One day we had a big signals scheme, in which my
section was engaged. I had a base station from which
communication was maintained by lamp across a valley.
Thence I ran a landline up a steep slope, with battalion
stations beyond. I was nervous throughout the show, as
I was constantly afraid my section would fail; but with
minor mishaps we didn't do so badly. It is true that as
the general, surrounded by his staff (myself shivering
with apprehension bringing up the rear), marched up the
line of communications, some fool in the front disturbed
my wire. It tightened across the path and just caught the
general under the chin. He was extraordinarily annoyed.

# Anzac Cove

The Anzac landing at Gallipoli – timed for dawn on 25 April 1915 to coincide with the landings at Cape Helles – began with a calamitous mistake. The troops spearheading the attack waded ashore on the wrong beach because the rowing-boats in which they were close-packed had been towed about a mile north of the intended target. Thus, the troops found themselves on a tiny beach overlooked by viciously steep hills that were pock-marked with gullies and ravines and well covered with spiny, gorse-like bushes. The uninviting terrain, far better suited to defence than to attack, became known to history as Anzac Cove, and on it some 15,000 Australians and New Zealanders were to create an imperishable legend….

There was no support for the landing from the big guns of battleships lying offshore. Lt General William Birdwood, Commander of the Anzacs, dispensed with the usual softening-up bombardment because he wanted and expected to take the Turks completely by surprise. In this belief he was not entirely justified, for a couple of hundred Turks, well concealed in the hillsides, had the first wave of the attack in the sights of their rifles and machine guns. The Turks were pushed back, but only after they had taken their toll on the Anzacs.

After consolidating their beachhead, the next objective of the Anzacs was to take the dominating high ground of the Sari Bair ridge – and they almost succeeded. What scuppered their chances was that Turkish reserves were only four miles away, under the command of a born soldier, Mustafa Kemal, who moved swiftly to stage a counter-attack. When Kemal berated a group of Turkish soldiers who were running away from the Anzacs, they told him they were out of ammunition. He ordered them to fix bayonets and lie down, facing the enemy. This halted the Anzac advance, and the struggle settled into a murderous rhythm of attack and counter-attack, with the Anzacs clinging on to their small gains.

The orders from General Hamilton, in overall charge of Allied operations at Gallipoli, were to 'dig, dig, dig'. This the Anzacs did, but they had more to contend with than the Turks. In summer they were plagued by heat, thirst and swarms of flies that brought dysentery and diarrhoea; in autumn, by torrents of rain; in winter, by debilitating frost-bite. As at Cape Helles, the Anzac landing ended in stalemate. Hamilton needed a master-stroke, and one that would be executed vigorously, if ever he was going to drive the Turks off Gallipoli.

I had a terrific dressing-down, and the old man was only appeased when I gave him a portable telephone down which he could bellow a message to the camp station. When he actually received the reply he was so aston-ished that my stock went up, although I realized that he regarded me and my signallers as an entirely incompe-tent outfit.

The days passed, and we received not one word as to future movements. I know, of course, that all the islands were full of spies, and that any indication of Command Staff's intentions might have been known straight away to the Turks, but I shall always think it was a mistake not to let divisions or even brigades know the nature of the task which awaited us, so that we could have prac-tised some of the manoeuvres which the new landing would necessitate. During this waiting period no one knew where, when or how the new thrust was to be made, even the divisional staff being kept in ignorance until a few days before zero time.

When the information did come, it was found that the expedition was a new landing accompanied by most complicated operations, and there had been no proper opportunity for practice or preparation.

The disease which ultimately played such havoc with me had made its appearance in the camp. There was hardly a man who had not already got diarrhoea of a most painful character. In my case I put it down to the flies, the infection probably being accentuated by too much bathing. I also believe that the sanitary arrangements were bad, having regard to the probability of such infection, for the open latrines swarmed with flies – ghastly clouds of them – and there was little enough attention to the water supply. We were always in trouble over water, for the supply was nowhere sufficient. You must realize that we were Englishmen who had never known real thirst, or ever the experience of being unable to quench what we knew of thirst. In addition, most of us had been accustomed to obtaining a ready flow by the turning of a mere tap, for there is little heard in England of contaminated water. We had not been on Imbros long, with its dry atmosphere and broiling day heat, before the troops knew the pangs of real thirst. And there was no adequate water on the island.

There was trouble. Everything else was forgotten in the craving for water. Water-carts had to be put under the charge of an armed guard, and officers spent their time in trying to wangle more water for their men. I actually found one crowd who had dug a small well, and were quietly supplying their own and neighbouring tents' needs, with water which must have been half sewage. I doubt whether the battalion staff officers had ever been given the elements of education as to sanitation, and the results were to be disastrous, for, as a wag put it: 'The XIth Division went into action grasping the rifle in one hand, and keeping up its trousers with the other.'

I had to go sick after a few days. My internal arrangements were giving me hell, and I could not eat anything. The MO gave me chlorodyne and talked vaguely about hospital. I went back to duty and took cold comfort in the fact that practically everyone else was in the same boat and trying to stick it out. But it was a bad start to such a show as Suvla Bay!

Sapper Y gave me some trouble in a very amusing way at Imbros. He turned up on parade unshaven and, when I told him off, claimed that King's Regulations permitted troops on active service to grow a beard! I ordered him to parade every morning half-an-hour before the rest of the section, at my tent, for my inspection of his shaven chin. I was acting as censor for my section, and Sapper Y had several lady correspondents to whom he swore undying and undivided love. He voiced his disapproval of my action in a letter which he well knew I should read! I wish I had that letter now, for it was a masterpiece.

'We have a queer officer in my section,' he wrote (as near as I can remember). 'I think he is a bit of a Piccadilly boy and he don't know his King's Regulations. He is trying to make me shave every morning and he knows that's not compelled by KR. Wait until I get him into the firing-line!'

I went with the brigade staff officers for a tour of the trenches in the peninsula. We were taken over from Imbros by a destroyer, and landed via the 'River Clyde'.[1] As I crossed its deck my thoughts were in the past; of the astonishing deeds of the 29th Division, the Colonial troops, and the Navy, in that almost impossible feat of forcing a landing in the face of a prepared and undisturbed enemy. The beaches were now organized wharves, with dugouts and shelters against the Turks' crossfire. I was distinctly relieved to find everything peaceful, for we had heard that, at times, the bombardment was very heavy.

Walking up the open country to the trenches with a guide, I suddenly heard a low whine gradually rising to a shriek, and a small shell burst in a field to our left. For the first time I was under fire. My ill-used stomach contracted even further, and certain painful symptoms, now becoming somewhat familiar, became distinctly manifest.

'It's no good trying to dodge them,' the brigade major remarked gently, as I ducked on the approach of another one. Since the shell burst at least a hundred yards away, I realized the force of the advice.

For some distance we had no cover, and the shelling increased – evidently the approach of a large party had been observed – so we spread out and before long we were in the trenches.

As a whole the trenches were badly constructed. At times, as we stumbled along, there was only slight protection from enfilading fire, and bullets seemed to be swarming round our heads. Of course, I was entirely without experience, so it all was much more terrifying than it would have been to the sophisticated. However I noticed that the general was not enjoying it either, which comforted me. The brigade major, on the other hand, seemed quite unmoved, and he had the capacity for giving out confidence, so I quickly came to rely on him.

We visited the front-line trenches, where the Turks were only a few yards away. I hated the appearance of our men. They were so grim and haggard, as if the blood had been drained from their faces, and expression from their eyes. Here would be a small party making a stew over an improvised fire, with clouds of flies surrounding everything; there a stretcher-party on the way to a distant call. We lunched with a battalion headquarters in a gully just behind the front line. As the Turks were as deficient as ourselves in howitzers, there was comparative protection in trenches and ravines. To me the meal was a melancholy affair, for a subaltern had just been killed in the front fire-trench, and his body, covered with a groundsheet, lay beside us as we ate. At that time the spirits of the troops were not very good. The operations had already become practically a stalemate, and there was small hope of breaking through to the Narrows. In addition, conditions for the Allied armies were very bad. There could be no rest for anyone on the Peninsula, for it was under constant fire from at least two sides. In fact it was almost more comfortable to be in the firing-line than at the rear; for shelling, especially with the heavies, was confined almost entirely to the beaches, while there was at least some cover in the trenches. I think the worst part was that there was no opportunity or period for rest. In France the conditions were, in many ways, infinitely worse than the East. There was gunfire in Europe the like of which we never experienced; there were attacks and counter-attacks perhaps more deadly than in Gallipoli; while in the line the troops must have had a much more hectic time than anything we had. Yet in France our armies had times of real, complete rest behind the lines; they had periods when the food was excellent, and water plentiful; they knew at least that they would be relieved at some time. In Gallipoli there was that hopeless feeling that no one could expect relief or rest. Everyone was doomed to stay there until death, disease or wounds overtook him. The best was a cushy wound, and even then rumour had it that he would get no nearer home than Malta. At the time of my visit to Helles, the average period of service in the peninsula for a subaltern was about thirty-six hours, so a certain degree of pessimism was understandable.

I can't say I learned a great deal from my little tour, but it depressed me pretty badly; and I first knew what it was like to have the complete and absolute wind up.

When we heard that Sir Ian Hamilton was going to inspect our Division, we guessed that we were soon to be on the move.

We paraded in our best turnout. I was stationed to one flank with my section at the head of the brigade. The troops looked simply magnificent, and I maintain that a finer selection of good British manhood will never be seen than those early Kitchener Armies.

Sir Ian Hamilton came slowly down the line, and came up to me.

'What were you before you joined the army?' he asked

me pleasantly. I told him that I had been a barrister.

'Do you like your new job?' he enquired in a thoughtful way, wondering perhaps how one could possibly expect to make a soldier out of such unpromising material!

The situation at Imbros was not conducive to a love for the General Staff. Stationed miles away on a comfortable ship, unseen and unheard of except through rumour, it was not surprising if the 'brass-hats' became unpopular. Stories floated round of luxurious living; and regimental officers who had to visit the ship, and who were, for instance, compelled to pay heavily for their lunch, hardly gave us glowing accounts. It was said that visits by staff officers to the peninsula were few and far between. I do not know how true these stories were, but they were to be expected, considering the negligible attempts which were made to inspire the troops with confidence in their leaders. I shall always think of Gallipoli as a campaign in which energetic leadership was an essential; in which the common soldiers had to be inspired with a belief in themselves, their objects,[2] and the capacity of their officers. We needed the glamour of a Napoleon, the respect for a Wellington, or the blind faith inspired by such a man as Cromwell. There was too little of that for us at any time in Gallipoli. My own general, with his divisional general, and accompanied by their corps general, all went home to England together. I can only say that my confidence in the brigade major was never shaken.

It was a curious coincidence, Bobby, that, just over a century earlier, your great-great-grandfather, then a midshipman in the Royal Navy, fought under Sir Sidney

Smith at the defence of Acre.[3] He was fighting with the Turks against the French and he would have been a little surprised if he had known that his great-grandson was to be allied to the French against the Turks – and fighting to obtain the same objectives as he lost three fingers in defending! You'll see many object lessons in this tale but I'm not going to draw any morals.

# 4

## FINAL PREPARATIONS

It was only before the Suvla Bay landing that Corps Headquarters issued any Operations Orders. Before these actual orders we had merely been informed that a landing was intended.

To my intense surprise the general told me that I was to be present at a conference of the Staff, in which the operations were to be explained and discussed. When I asked the reason I was told that upon me had fallen a very difficult task, which would be explained in due course.

Feeling like a fly buzzing into the throne-room of a king, I was duly taken by the brigade major to the meeting. Apart from the staff officers there was no regimental officer of a rank lower than lieutenant-colonel, so my solitary pip seemed out of place. I listened carefully as the general operations were explained, following meanwhile the long printed instructions which had been handed round.

There was to be a new landing at Suvla Bay and the coast adjacent. The landing was to be a surprise, so that no artillery preparation would precede it, and success depended entirely on the troops making a speedy advance and consolidating their position on certain natural features before the Turks could bring up their reserves. It was anticipated that the landing would be unopposed, and no difficulty was expected over the actual disembarkation. We then heard that special lighters had been constructed for transporting the troops to the beaches, each one capable of carrying half a battalion. These were to be towed over by destroyers until the coast was reached, when the lighters would be cast off, to make their own way to the shore under their auxiliary engines. It was expected that the lighters would be able to run close inshore, so that the troops would be able to land without getting wet.

On disembarkation, each brigade of the division had its own objective. The official history of the expedition gives details, so I do not propose to deal with them now except so far as my own brigade was concerned. We had to land actually in Suvla Bay itself, just north of the mouth of a small streamlet, where the beach shelved steeply to a sandy beach. Battalions were to march in lines of companies, and a position marked on the maps as Hill 10 was our immediate objective.

Then I heard what my own particular job was to be. My orders were that, immediately on landing, I was to establish a station on the beach, leaving an operator there. Then I was to follow the advancing infantry, laying a telephone line until our objective had been attained, when another station was to be established. It was laid down that in the landing no lights were to be shown and no noise made, even talking being prohibited. The advance by the lines of infantry was to be at the rate of two miles per hour, at which speed the telephone line had to be laid in order to keep touch with the advance. No indication was given of the country over which my line had to be laid: I did not know whether it was rough rocks, or fields and pastureland.

I was too concerned with my own part in the expedition to take much notice of anything else. It was impressed upon me that, so far as the landing at Suvla was concerned, I was really the connecting link between the infantry in their advance, the beach, and the supporting fleet. It was even suggested that I could receive messages from the ships either by lamp or helio but, considering the capacity of my signallers, I had little hope of it. It struck me as somewhat surprising that a brigade signal section should be given such a task at all, or that a subaltern should have so much responsibility. I did not mind the latter, provided we could do the job, but frankly I thought we could never get it done. It is no easy matter laying a telephone line by hand, even under the best conditions. The drums of wire are carried by hand, the wire being paid out as required and fixed in position on hedges or along ditches. If the wire gets caught up it must be disentangled, and the various numbers on the several duties have to work in close co-operation to avoid confusion. How all this was to be done in pitch darkness, without noise or talking, passed my comprehension, especially over country of which we had no knowledge.

I wondered whether the orders to the infantry were of a similarly complicated character. Although I heard no criticism at the pow-wow, the various COs of the battalions looked very worried, and it did not take a very well-trained military mind to grasp that if units were to be landed at so many points on the coast, and were to work to complicated time-schedules, something might easily go wrong with the whole show. It was like a prepared scheme of attack in chess – except that there was no provision for any move by the opponent! And any unexpected move might throw the whole scheme into chaos. Think of the various units, without any inter-communication, landing at different places down the coast in darkness; imagine them making for objectives which they had only seen on a map. Such evolutions could be achieved under some conditions, but it was foredoomed to failure if there was any opposition: when some advances might be held up; when time schedules might go wrong, or contingents get wiped out.

My ever-present trouble at Imbros led me to take particular notice of the arrangement for the supply of water: '*Water will be found on the mainland.*'[1] Considering the fact that we had never had our bellies full of water since we had landed at Imbros, I was not heartened by this optimistic forecast. I have never forgotten the phrase, for the reality made it into something like a sardonic sneer.

My own staff were under no illusions as to the difficulties of their own job, or of mine in particular. We had as difficult a landing as any unit: right in Suvla Bay itself, with a salt lake on our right, the nature of which – whether dry or marshy – we knew nothing. Our objective was the aforementioned feature marked on the plan as Hill 10,[2] but how we were to know when we had arrived at such a doubtful spot no one could say.

I was thoroughly miserable about my orders, for I did not believe it was possible to lay a telephone line by hand, in the dark, without talking, at the speed of two miles an hour; and I was quite sure that if I once lost touch with the advancing infantry, I was as likely to reach Constantinople as Hill 10.

The general decided very wisely that we must have a rehearsal. We obtained the use of one of the lighters and arranged a night landing on a selected beach not far from the camp. I told my section what was expected of us, and they took it very philosophically. Meanwhile we overhauled our stores, especially the drums of wire, on the behaviour of which so much would depend.

It was a pitch-black night when we marched down to the sea. We found our lighter all ready: a quaint-looking craft of large dimensions made of iron, like a long shallow bath-tub, with an engine astern. A whole battalion had already been taken aboard and the general with his staff officers joined them.

We slowly *chug-chugged* down the coast, only the outline of the hills being visible. We displayed no lights, and no orders or talking were allowed.

I am afraid that I started fussing even on the lighter, wondering whether all the stores were safe, and whether my section had kept together. I was anxious to put up a good performance, for I had been living for months with regular soldiers, chaffingly referred to as 'the civvy'; and now I was to be tested. Yet I still doubted whether we could carry out our orders. I could not help wondering whether a regular RE subaltern would have funked it.

Our weird vessel suddenly slewed round, and we found ourselves gradually approaching the shore. The bottom of the lighter grated, and then we grounded heavily. Ahead was a steeply shelving beach, on which a collapsible platform could be lowered from the bows of the lighter, allowing the troops to disembark dry-shod.

The beach was very narrow, with high banks barely a dozen paces from the water. Here the infantry fell in, still in complete silence, while I made hasty preparations. As I explained earlier, the laying of a telephone line is done by men known by numbers, who each have their special duties. One number carries the drum, [that] one pays it out, while a third places it in position on the ground, or along hedges and ditches. To get a good start it was essential that each man should be ready with his stores or tools, and in the meantime an operator had to fix up a 'station' on the beach, from which the line was to be laid.

Almost before we were ready there was a muttered word from the front, a sudden movement, and we were off.

The very worst happened – for the infantry were immediately swallowed up by the darkness. It was so dark that I momentarily lost touch even with my own section, in the rear of which I was stumbling.

'Troops will advance at two miles an hour,' I thought bitterly; for our start had been like that of a hundred-yard race.

I found the section hurrying along, tearing the cable off the drums, and leaving it on the ground to take care of itself. In time we caught the infantry, who had halted, and took a breather. Then once again we went away. There came an awful tangle in the wire, and all the pretence at silence went by the board, and sibilant curses broke out. I would have given a good deal to strike even a match, for I defy anyone to disentangle telephone wire in pitch darkness.

We left a glorious knot behind and rushed after the infantry, now Lord knew where. Fortunately there had been another check, and we had a few minutes to straighten up and recover our equilibrium.

I had the ridiculous idea that I was understudying Harry Tate or Will Evans,[3] for our muttered language and wild efforts would have provoked the laughter of the gods. First it would be the drum which wouldn't unwind, then some idiot would find the wire round his leg – or, worse, his neck – and all the time there was the fear that the silent line of infantry would suddenly leap away into the void.

That's exactly what did happen. Without any warning, and at quite five miles an hour, the whole line suddenly bolted into the night. Desperately, we followed. We fell over rocks and through scrubby bushes, the whole section pouring with sweat. In five minutes I knew we had lost the infantry altogether. We could not possibly keep up such a rate, and I went forward at a more leisurely speed, hoping to catch up at the next halt. I had been given a map with route and objective marked, but it was impossible to see it, since lights were forbidden, instructions being to use the compass.

We halted and listened, but there was not a sound. Inky blackness surrounded us, and each man had a different idea as the direction to take. I tried to take a bearing with the compass, and we set off again.

On we went until the dawn broke. I then saw our situation with respect to the camp, but not a sign of the infantry we were supposed to follow. After a considerable time of fruitless search we packed up and marched back to camp. A complete failure, I knew. I told the brigade major of our difficulties, and he was sympathetic; but the general was very angry.

'The whole show was for your benefit, and you have hopelessly failed,' was the epitome of the telling-off I got.

It was decided to repeat the test the same night. I received much advice and a stern warning. Did I not realize that the whole brigade's safety might depend on my line of communication?

Once again we marched down to the shore and embarked on the lighter. The night, if anything, was blacker than before, and our spirits were lower than ever. I now believed that our task was an impossibility, unless we had the most prodigious luck, and I was furious that no one could apparently appreciate the difficulties. It was such bad luck to come to grief before we had heard a shot fired, and before we had had a reasonable test.

Once again we fixed up the operator on the beach, and waited quietly for the infantry to move off.

The next move would have been funny if it had not been tragic; for the whole line of infantry simply leapt forward and disappeared. I don't know whether they actually *ran*, but that's what it seemed like. We rushed after them. I was at the rear, determined that there should be no tangles. Suddenly I heard a smothered curse from the front. Rushing forward I found myself falling, and I precipitately joined the wretched man with the drum who had fallen headlong down the bank of a ravine. We sorted out ourselves, our instruments, and the clinging coils of wire, with the assistance of several prohibited matches, and much blasphemy.

I will cut short an unhappy episode. We never saw the advancing infantry again. It must be remembered that a fractional error in the compass bearing at the start could be fatal. As dawn came we stood alone on the arid waste, bruised and fed-up. I was suddenly seized with furious anger at the futility of it all, and I ordered the section straight back to camp. Personally I went to bed. The expedition was not back, so the general was still apparently waiting for me, but I was quite indifferent to the consequences.

I was duly hauled out of my tent to face the general, and he was livid with rage. I guess that in most armies I would have been court-martialled, and I should certainly have been relieved of my job if there had been time to get another officer to take my place, for the general told me so with many flowery embellishments of speech.

I fancy the brigade major was more understanding, but he gave me no sympathy because I had retired to bed! The following day I got the general into a better frame of mind, for I rescued him from a centipede which attacked him in his bed. I can see him now, dancing about in his night attire and wildly yelling for '*Flags!*'

# The Last Throw

The Allied troops at Cape Helles and Anzac Cove, far from driving the Turks off Gallipoli, had not, despite their bravery, gained much ground. But an admission of failure would have been a heavy blow to Britain's prestige, especially among the millions of Muslims within the embrace of the Empire. So the Dardanelles Committee in London took a fateful decision. General Hamilton would be reinforced and a massive new attack would be launched at Suvla Bay, a few miles to the north of Anzac Cove. This move was to coincide with an Anzac assault against the heights of Sari Bair.

The general chosen by Kitchener for this task was the 61-year-old Sir Frederick Stopford, who had never commanded troops in battle and was plucked from a ceremonial post at the Tower of London because his name came high up in the army's seniority list. Hamilton muttered feebly and ineffectively against the choice, but Kitchener was never going to release an experienced officer from the killing grounds of France. And Hamilton was never going to stand up to Kitchener.

The Turkish leadership were taken by surprise when men of General Stopford's IX Corps, part of Kitchener's New Army, put ashore at Suvla in the night of 6 August. A few sentries fired off shots, but soon fled. However, there was utter confusion on the beach, with men wandering around in the darkness, trying to find their units. A major British objective after dawn was to capture the Anafarta Ridge, less than half a dozen miles from the shore, but General Frederick Hammersley, commanding the attack, had no reliable maps, no heavy artillery support and no idea of how many Turks were lying in wait.

# 5

## THE LANDING AT SUVLA BAY

The day came: the 6th August 1915. At last Kitchener's Army was to be tried out. Ten months of
training for me, and then the real article.

Already it was apparent to the simplest mind that our
training had been defective. The division had received
the usual barrack-square drill, had fired its musketry
courses, and been hardened by PT and route marches.
But all this was under home conditions, including the
mild climate of England. We knew and had been told
nothing of open fighting amid the arid wastes of a
semi-tropical country. We could not curb our thirst, nor
were we used to iron rations. Of the heat of the broiling day, followed by the chill of the dark nights, we had
already had a taste, but we could not guess the strain of
it under fighting conditions. Except for a handful in the
division, officers and men had never heard a shot fired
in anger, and there was to be no gradual baptism of fire
as in France. And finally there was scarcely an officer
or man who was not affected by dysentery or colic. I
believe that if the division (and this applies to all the

troops in the expedition) had not been so keen to put up a good show, half the strength would have gone sick at Imbros. As it was there was a big run on the chlorodyne, just to get a quietus for the big attack.

There were no reviews, nor harangues to the troops. Neither the corps nor divisional generals could find anything of encouragement or advice to say. We embarked in an atmosphere quite devoid of excitement or enthusiasm. When the 29th Division and Colonials left for Helles, there were wonderful scenes of enthusiasm, but I remember nothing except a grim air of determination mixed with a sense of fatality. The day had come, and we had to get on with the job. There were crowds to see us off, but I felt no reaction except to the correspondents who were busy with their cameras, and some contempt for the Base details and 'brass-hats' who were staying behind. I don't think we missed anything in the send-off, for we were not used to enthusiasm since leaving England, and anyway it is awfully difficult to be gay when you have a chronic stomach-ache.

I embarked with the brigade staff officers in the destroyer *Beagle* with two battalions: the 8th Northumberland Fusiliers and the 5th Dorsetshire Regiment. We were towing a lighter filled with troops of various battalions. We crept away in the gloom towards the shores of Gallipoli.

This is the proper moment to give a dissertation on one's feelings when going into action. Was I frightened? The answer is an emphatic affirmative: terribly scared – of all sorts of things. I was afraid of sudden annihilation, of lingering death, and of making a mess of my job, and I had the horror for the unknown. Would our landing be unopposed as expected, or was it to be a repetition of Cape Helles? Would civilian soldiers be able to stand the test?

As we steamed slowly along, it suddenly seemed as if a volcano on the horizon had burst into flames, spreading further every moment. Then came the boom of guns. We were gazing at the battlefields of Gallipoli, silhouetted in flame.

The scene heartened me. The bombardment was terrific – surely no man could stand against it, and our path would be easy? As we approached, it seemed that the whole peninsula was clothed in fire, the effect being similar to a magnificent firework exhibition at the Crystal Palace, seen from a distance. I thought of our comrades who were making a great attack, so we were told, to draw attention from our landing. They were now chancing their lives in the great adventure, and one felt the itch to be there alongside. Not much bravery in that, but comradeship, and something of determination to carry out the appointed task. My section were with me on deck, eagerly watching the scene. They were quiet but self-controlled; and I saw no sign of fear.

In due course, the officers of the destroyer gave us an excellent spread in the mess. All the officers were there, comprising the general, his staff, and the battalion officers. We sat at a big oval table, the general and staff being to my left. Something of the melodrama of the scene struck me forcibly, so that it is one of the most vivid memories left to me: of the quietness of the room, with the subdued chatter of neighbours, all oppressed by the quickly advancing fate prepared for each one of us. I glanced to my right, where the regimental officers were gathered. I wondered how many of them would be alive in – say – four hours; and my thoughts turned to myself. Was this my last night?

I almost had a bet with myself in a whimsical fashion, even going so far as counting the faces round me to be included in the odds which fate might wager. About twelve there were to the right of me; good stout fellows who were mostly friends of mine, from the young sub-altern who had barely left school, now smiling (what effort that smile cost, who knows?) – at the big major beside him, to the brigade machine-gun officer almost opposite me. The big major was second in command of the battalion, famous as much for the largeness of his heart as the size of his posterior. It was the opinion of the battalion that no Turkish rifleman could miss that protuberance, and that no cover would be sufficient to protect the natural feature referred to!

I thought of that bet afterwards, on a day to be referred to, when we were withdrawn to the beach after four days continuous fighting. Every single man who had been included in my fantastic bet was missing from the roll-call.

We stumbled out on deck to find that the outline of the shore was now dimly discernible. Away to our right the infernal racket of the several battles was still being waged, a blaze of intermittent flashes marking shell explosions, the air vibrating with the detonations. A few hundred yards away were the Anzac beaches, while further to the south was Cape Helles. In front of us lay the unknown Suvla Bay, now dark and quiet.

In deep silence we saw the lighter which we had been towing cast adrift. A faint *chug-chug* marked the starting of its engine, and it slowly drifted away towards the beach. We now anchored about three or four hundred yards out, for we were to wait while the lighter reached the shore, when it would discharge its cargo and return for us. You can imagine our excitement now, as we imagined it approaching its destination. We reckoned it would take about fifteen minutes to reach the shore, and we listened with bated breath for any sign of opposition.

There was a sudden crackle of rifle fire right ahead of us along the coast. Flashes appeared at different spots.

The landing had been discovered!

There was nothing worse in the whole of the Gallipoli show for me than the subsequent wait. We could see nothing of the movements of our first contingent, and the lighter did not return for us for hours. In the meantime the coast in front of us had blazed into life, and spent bullets were soon whistling round our ears. We knew that the infantry were forbidden to fire their rifles until dawn, and thus the whole of the noise came from the Turks. It did not look as if we were to be exactly unopposed.

A distant whine, a big splash, and a shell dropped alongside our destroyer. It's a nasty feeling being cooped up with nothing to be done about it.

At long last, about half-past three, back came the lighter. We heard that something had gone wrong with the navigation of our destroyer, for we had missed our proper place of disembarkation by a wide margin, with the result that, instead of the lighter being able to discharge its troops directly on to the beach, it had unexpectedly grounded nearly a hundred yards out on rocks. The men had been compelled to swim or wade in, while others had got ashore on small boats. The lighter had had the greatest difficulty in getting off the rocks. Evidently someone else had been unable to get a good compass bearing in the dark!

We quickly dropped into the lighter – jammed in like sardines. This time we went very cautiously for the shore, for the officer in charge had no intention of going aground again. As the strange vessel moved slowly in, the firing from the shore increased, and the ping of bullets proved that we were the direct target. A subdued cry, and the sagging of the massed men close at hand spoke of a casualty. Others followed, yet the lighter made exasperatingly slow progress.

My mouth was dry, and my stomach seemed bound with steel hoops. At last I knew the feeling of stark fear.

Our first wish was to get out of that lighter. Penned up there without cover, we looked even at the sea with longing.

The bottom of the lighter suddenly scraped on shoals. The engine stopped. Looking ahead we still could not see the actual beach. How far out were we?

A hail from the side, and there appeared a number of rowing boats. Into these we clambered. I tried to keep my section together, and to see that we got our instruments ashore, but in the end we had to get away as best as we could.

In a few minutes the beach came into view, some thirty yards or so away, and at the same time our over-crowded boat grounded. The air seemed full of bullets, and all around were the cries of the wounded.

With a warning to keep the instruments dry, I put a

leg over the side of the boat, and dropped into the sea. Slipping on the side of a slimy rock I went straight into deepish water. Recovering myself, I found the occupants of my boat all around, slipping, stumbling, and cursing. You'll know how difficult it is to walk along the rocks on the seashore even at low tide, so you'll guess what it meant to wade along in the dark, over slimy rock and through deep pools, with bullets whistling round one's head. I never expected to reach the shore. My mind was numb, and my limbs would scarcely function. No instinct was left except to keep on doing something, and as one couldn't run away, forward it must be.

I was almost surprised when I came to the dry sand, and I hurled myself down. With a jerk I remembered my section, and Operation Orders, and rose to my feet to survey the beach.

A short distance away, the shore seemed alive with the dim forms of men apparently running in different directions and sometimes in circles, without aim or object. I then found that, at some points, the enemy had not yet been driven off and was putting up a vigorous resistance. Further along the shore were crowds of troops just landed who were in the process of sorting themselves out to their units, for our brigade staff had been delayed by hours in the landing, so that while some units had already started to carry out their operation orders, others had not yet been disembarked.

I fortunately stumbled over my section sergeant with a few of the men who were lying flat on the beach. He and I walked up and down collecting the rest of the section, and soon we had them lying down in lines. Stores were in a bad way, as many of the instruments were soaked with salt water, while much cable and other material had been abandoned. I was not surprised to hear also that some bicycles, which we had been ordered to take ashore, were also missing.

I had my first bad blow then. My sergeant, a most capable fellow, was discussing the position with me. We were standing face to face, my back to the field of the enemy fire, when the sergeant dropped at my feet, with a bullet through his kneecap. How that bullet could have hit him without touching me will be an everlasting mystery, and I think it must have passed between my legs.

Escape number one!

I now had a doubled responsibility, but fortunately I had an efficient corporal who promptly took over his senior's duties, and we fixed up the section, with the stores and instruments, under a sandbank to await developments.

In the meantime there was renewed fighting just beyond us. In the intense darkness which preceded the dawn one could just discern groups of men in every direction, some apparently engaged in hand-to-hand fighting. The rifle fire was now intense and an occasional shell would explode. I dully wondered what had become of the scheme of operations, and of my orders to lay a telephone behind a line of advancing infantry!

I walked a short distance along the beach and discovered the general anxiously discussing the situation with the brigade major, and reported myself. I found that we must have landed far to the south of our intended starting point, and that no one could say even the direction of our objective, Hill 10. It was, however, obvious that we must move along the beach to the north, and I went back for my section.

The men were safe under their bank, but I routed them out. I soon began to find out those who were to be relied upon under fighting conditions. One man who was excellent under training would be simply palsied under fire, while another who had always been in my bad books would be as cool as a cucumber. I soon noticed my unshaven friend Sapper Y. He was one of the first away from the bank, ready for that dash along the beach which was now being sprayed with bullets. My best telephonist – a quiet boy with nice manners – seemed rooted to the ground, and I saw his bosom friend dragging at him. They ran along the beach together for a few yards, and then the boy dropped with a bullet through his throat.

We hurried along the beach pursued by that devastating hail of lead. A sunken riverbed, which in rainy weather drained the salt lake behind the bay, barred our progress, but we waded through it. It is curious that many writers have said that the bed was dry, but I have a distinct recollection of the stream, the water running nearly up to my waist, and it occurred to me at the time that one does not often get a ducking both from salt and fresh water twice in an hour.

The general and brigade major had found a large sand-hill which rose about ten feet high, just behind the beach proper, continuing in broken hillocks for some distance inland. It was still dark, although the eastern sky was lightening. I thought we had reached our objective, Hill 10, and I believe that the general was under the same impression. Even when the dawn broke we saw no real feature of the country which could be the proper Hill 10, and it was not for a long time that I was aware of the mistake. In any event we remained in the comparative security of the bank; I fixed my signal station there, and the projected march inland with me laying a telephone line in the rear came to nothing. I wasted no tears over that disappointment!

# 6

# THE DAWN

Daybreak found the brigade staff with about half the strength of one battalion still sheltering under the protection of the sand dunes to the north of Suvla Bay.

A tremendous surprise awaited us, for the bay was crowded with shipping. Where we had landed from a solitary destroyer there was now every type of warship imaginable, from the small sweeper to the mighty monitor. Transports, provision ships and huge warships seemed to extend to the horizon. A beautiful white hospital ship lay close inshore.

I was standing on the beach gazing at this wonderful display when there was a sudden ear-splitting crash; the world and my brain stood still in paralysed shock. Yet another roar on the Turkish hills – the monitor was in action, throwing its huge shells over our heads. Other warships followed, and a terrific bombardment began.

It was wonderfully heartening to us, for we did not know then that the guns were doing little damage. To us it seemed that nothing could stand against such a metal hurricane.

I wonder, in parentheses, whether it will ever be explained why the Navy had such confidence in their fleet guns. To the lay mind it would appear obvious that a gun with a flat trajectory could only be effective against troops in the open, and that the Turks had only to take cover behind natural features of the country – and Gallipoli was deeply scarred with hillocks and ravines – to be practically immune. It is all the more remarkable inasmuch as the Navy had already failed once, for the terrific bombardment which preceded the landing at Cape Helles did not dislodge the Turks even from their entrenchments, while it had no effect on the reserves sheltering in the hills. One howitzer would have been more effective than half-a-dozen other guns of any calibre; yet I never saw one of them.

Despite the support from the sea, our position on the beach was precarious. As I have explained, our own brigade scheme of advance had broken down, whether because of a mistake over the position of Hill 10, or because the several hours' delay in disembarkation had disorganized the staff plans. This advance was to have been undertaken by one battalion, with the brigade staff; but we were now, as I have said, still under the sand dunes on the fringe of the beach.

Of the other brigades of the division, one was to make the landing south of Lala Baba, with orders to capture the fortified post on the prominence, and then to sweep along the beach, round the salt lake, to the attack on Chocolate Hill,[1] which, with Ismail Oglu Tepe, commanded the valley of the salt lake as well as the valley leading through the hills to the east.

Another battalion landed north of the bay, with

orders to clear the hills known as Kiretch Tepe Sirt.

At daybreak, therefore, we eagerly sought news of our other battalions. The infantry could now use their rifles and the din was terrific, but for a time it was almost impossible to get any information.

Presently a staff officer came along the beach, and various stragglers joined our headquarters, so that we heard the tale of the landing of other units, and received fresh instructions.

It was an amazing story we were told, coloured according to the character of the teller. We heard of landings almost unopposed at one spot, of barbed wire and landmines in another. Where plans had gone right, the infantry had attacked with great verve, but casualties, especially amongst the officers, had been very serious. The attack on the post at Lala Baba had resulted in the loss of the CO of the battalion, along with several other senior officers, and the Turks had defended themselves with great determination and bravery. Incidentally, the attack had been delayed here while the Turks had been cleared up, and the same tale was told everywhere. This delay was not the only trouble, for the preliminary fighting had already caused exhaustion and some confusion.

Looking to the north, one could see the low range of hills in which one of our battalions was still engaged. There was heavy fire from that direction, but no message could be got through, since the Turks still occupied the low-lying country between the beach and the northern hills, including that Hill 10 which we could now locate, and which we ought to have captured at the first advance. There can be little doubt that, if our objective had been attained, we would have been linked up with

-63-

it was I loaded my revolver, and waited for the first Turk to put his head over the top of the dune. If such a head had appeared I have no doubt that I should have missed it by feet!

Our infantry were now lining the fringe of the sand banks *Keeping up a steady fire* blazing back at the Turks, but the latter seemed to be getting nearer. With the waves rolling in some few yards behind us there was no question of retreat.

A cheer broke out, and there, coming along the beach at the double, came long lines of supports, being the units which had attacked Lala Baba, who were now skirting the Salt Lake with Chocolate Hill as their final objective. They joined up with our *half* battalion, and the Turkish force melted away, probably content with having made a mere demonstration. Further waves of infantry continued to arrive, and The second phase of the battle began with a drive to the east, *which at last we completed the real thrill to.*

Now began a period in which I could either hash up the final history as pieced together in the official records, or could give you my own confused impressions and memories. The two standpoints are totally dissimilar. At the time I had no idea of the tactical scheme, *no idea* of what was happening on other fronts, and only a hazy idea even of the positions of the battalions comprising the Brigade for which I was responsible. During that worst of all days, the 7th July, I lived in a sort of nightmare. Unbelievable things kept on happening and I gave up any attempt to determine what was a fact and what was false. Some things I experienced myself, others were told to me by credible people, while fantastic stories were

Part of the original manuscript in which Arthur Beecroft describes the events of the morning of 7 August 1915 (see pages 93–4)

the right wing of the battalion on Kiretch Tepe Sirt, and with the left wing of the troops attacking Chocolate Hill.

As soon as the light was strong enough, the Turks saw the disposition of the armies, and we got our first taste of real gunfire. The shells were mostly of small size, the enemy having brought up mountain and field guns into the hills overlooking the bay, but the targets were easy and our casualties correspondingly heavy.

We did not feel particularly cheerful, for we did not know what was happening, and we had that disturbing feeling that things had been bungled. So far as our part was concerned we had good reason for our doubts. In addition, we had had a rare soaking and our clothes had dried on us. Troops had landed in light order without overcoats, and the night air had chilled us to the bone. I had on a uniform made of some ridiculous material recommended in London which protected me from neither sun nor cold.

Just after dawn a heavy fusillade broke out directly ahead, and from a comparatively short distance. The Turks appeared to be counter-attacking. I know now that it was a brave feint by a small company of the enemy, but at the time we thought it was a determined effort to drive us into the sea. That was the moment when I regretted that I was a sapper, for I could do so little. It is true that a sapper friend of mine in France gained the MC for leading a counter-attack armed only with a portable telephone which he swung round his head with disastrous result for the enemy, but that cannot be recommended as a general weapon of offence. As it was, I loaded my revolver and waited for the first

Turk to put his head over the top of the dune. If such a head had appeared I have no doubt that I would have missed it by feet!

Our infantry were now lining the fringe of the sandbanks, keeping up a steady fire at the Turks, but the latter seemed to be getting nearer. With the waves rolling in some few yards behind us there was no question of retreat.

A cheer broke out, and there, coming along the beach at the double, appeared lines of supports, being the units which had attacked Lala Baba, who were now skirting the salt lake with Chocolate Hill as their final objective. They joined up with our half battalion, and the Turkish force melted away, probably content with having made a mere demonstration. Further waves of infantry continued to arrive. The second phase of the battle had begun, with a drive to the east, in which at last we captured the real Hill 10.

Now began a period in which I could either hash up the final history as pieced together in the official records, or could give you my own confused impressions and memories. The two standpoints are totally dissimilar. At the time I had no information as to the tactical scheme, no news of what was happening on other fronts, and only a hazy idea even of the positions of the battalions comprising the brigade, for which I was responsible. During the worst of all days, the 7th August, I lived in a sort of nightmare. Unbelievable things kept on happening and I gave up any attempt to determine what was a fact and what was false. Some things I experienced myself, others were told to me by credible people, while fantastic stories were repeated which may or may not have been true.

One of the most extraordinary stories, which I believe is nevertheless true, was that one battalion, attacking north from Lala Baba, came to a strongly held hillock. A prolonged and sanguinary engagement with the bayonet ensued, when it was suddenly discovered that the position was held by our own troops. Here was an appalling example of the result of complicated operations in the dark over unknown country, to which I have already referred.

I think you will want to hear about the battle as it appeared to me, however, and so I will try to give only my own experiences.

For some time my signal station remained at the pseudo-Hill 10, in other words the sand dune on the beach. There remained the general and the brigade major, and messages reporting the progress of our brigade came in all day. It was almost impossible to keep in touch with units, for the battle was constantly swaying in all directions. I would get a position at one moment and find it different within a few minutes. From the battalion on the northern hills I had no message at all, although they got a message through the fleet to divisional HQRS.

By ten o'clock the beach was swarming with fresh troops, with stores, ammunition, and guns. The confusion on that short and narrow beach was appalling, while the target for the Turkish guns was almost unmissable. I had a very close squeak early that morning. Some of my section were standing idle and were detailed to carry up ammunition boxes. Two of them, holding a long box by its slings, came to report their departure, and I was standing beside them. A distant whine rose to a roar and crash, as a shell fell between us and directly under the box of ammunition.

It never exploded: it was a dud! Escape number two!

The two men dropped that box, then looked at me with white faces. We decided to laugh – a rather forced laugh – about it! As they moved off I took a long look at the shell, now buried some distance in the sand. It seemed incredible luck. Perhaps I wasn't going to be killed after all. One gets superstitious very quickly under sudden-death conditions. I once gazed at the life-line on my hand, and wondered whether there was not a break in it! Then, when one had to cross an open stretch of country, would come the question 'Now, or a second later? It may make all the difference.' Such ideas would recur however one fought them, until the time came of desperate indifference to one's fate.

General Haggard of the next brigade in our division came to pay us a visit with the whole of his staff. He was a man entirely without fear, and would stroll about under heavy fire with the utmost nonchalance, much to the consternation of his staff. On this occasion he was under a sandbank just beyond my station so that, by looking round a corner of my own bank, I could see him. The shriek of an approaching shell gave us warning, and I have dim memories of ignominiously hurling myself on to the sand as the shell appeared to be making for my head. There was a roar of its burst, and clouds of fumes and sand. How close to me it had been I cannot say, but it took off the general's leg and nearly wiped out his staff.

In spite of our early tribulations, the courage of the troops was excellent. You will have read ridiculous tales of how the infantry had to be prodded into battle; of officers who stopped runaways with their revolvers; of the horror of the sensitive man who cannot face the terror of death. I saw little of this sort of thing. Our troops, in spite of their embryonic training, were determined to make good. Discipline was good, because it arose from a sense of comradeship. There were cases where individuals and even battalions broke and ran back, but they were collected again and soon recovered their proper spirit without recourse to force.

I went up eastwards with the advancing infantry later in the morning, and the ground was sprinkled with our dead and wounded. One of the first I found was the brigade machine-gun officer. Shrapnel had made a terrible mess of his leg, and he had bled to death.

We went some distance inland, and our troops appeared to be making good progress. Yet the real troubles of the day began to show themselves: heat and thirst. The former was terrific, not so much in degrees as the way in which it seemed to *strike* into one. But the thirst was unbelievable unless one had experienced it. We had our full bottles for the landing, and nothing else. It was impossible not to take little sips from time to time, so that gradually the bottles were emptied. Then came raging thirst.

'*Water will be found on the mainland.*' It is true there were wells, but some had been deliberately contaminated, while others were marked to the inch by Turkish sharp-shooters. Corpses were piled around the edges of the wells, yet there were many more crazed men ready to risk their lives – they said they would rather die of a bullet than go mad through thirst. And there were many who became mad, and staggered about with consciousness gone from their eyes. Those who fought on had blackened lips and swollen tongues, and occasionally for all of us the sky and the dry earth would reel dizzily.

Man made in the image of God can soon revert to the likeness of an animal. A hunted look comes to the eyes; the pallor of nerve-strain appears even through the sweat of midday; and there is the lustful cruelty as bayonet is rammed home. I saw all this for four continuous days, yet never forgot the magnificence of the courage of those civilian soldiers, and of their grand sense of duty and comradeship to each other. Officers and men shared alike, tasting the same hell, united alike in effort and death.

At any moment I'm likely to get prosy, but that's the privilege of a father! I wanted to tell you about my own funk, too! You see, one gets so tired of expecting to be killed all the time. You'd like to get it over, yet in the meantime there's work to be done. With one part of your brain you write a message, or adjust a telephone, while the other side is registering the fact that that last *'ping'* must have been damned close to your head. Or you are walking up to the line – frightfully scared – and you see some wretched lad who is gibbering with the same sensation as yourself, and you grin amiably at him, trying to give the debonair impression that you didn't mind if it hailed shells. And if you can see him push on again more cheerfully, it's not too bad, and you get a bit more pluck yourself.

Something of resignation comes after a time – the old idea of only dying once, *kismet*, hell-to-it-but let's-get-on-with-it! The only trouble is that every really close squeak makes you realize how much you want to live.

Example is the best aid. If you see a really cool man you seem to acquire something of his fortitude, and his attitude shakes up your own self-respect. The brigade major was my sheet anchor, for he remained always steady. That he suffered was obvious from his appearance, but he never lost self-control. I remember one night when we were having a cat-nap in a small ravine, and I knew that I would have to leave its safety for a certain purpose – the umpteenth time – and I lay there with my stomach growling, wondering how I could ever face the sniper who had got a rifle fixed on our position. You'll say it was not much of a risk, but if you heard the bullets cracking overhead with monotonous regularity, you'd understand. I had to go, and I crept back through the scrub about twenty yards, and those bullets seemed to follow me all the way. Coming back the sharpness of one sound told me of a very close call, and I panicked. I tumbled into the ravine, almost on to the prostrate figure of the brigade major.

'Now then!' came the sharp exclamation. 'Pull yourself up, Flags! That won't do!'

In a moment I had recovered. In another, we were laughing over a mere episode. But I didn't forget it next day.

I am digressing hopelessly, for I was telling you of that momentous day, the 7th August, of the attacks which were made along the line, and of the difficulties we had to face. It has always been said quite truly that the seventh was a crucial day, for, if we had obtained our objectives, the Turks would have been compelled to retire, and their armies in the south would have had their communications cut. It has also been said, however, that the Suvla Bay force never pushed home the attack at all – it has even been asserted that, for a time, the troops sat tight and did nothing at all.

Time was lost, it is true, and the battle was thereby lost, but there were plenty of reasons for it. Those early hours on the beaches in desperate fighting, the severity of which has never been fully appreciated; the appalling confusion on the beaches later on; the absence of proper orders owing to the confusion and to lack of real leadership; and the physical condition of the troops to which I have referred, all produced their effect. The fact was that we were nearly done in even by the afternoon of that day, so we had not the physical power to push home any attack, even though the opposition was weak. If – always that *if* – fresh troops could then have taken up the battle, the story of Gallipoli might have had a different ending.

As it was, although we had no proper rations, practically no water, and were nearly unconscious from fatigue, we were called upon to fight continuously for three more days.

For a long time I could get no news of our battalion up in the Kiretch Tepe Sirt. It is noteworthy that although a message was sent to the Navy by helio reporting progress, I never got it. To send a runner there seemed hopeless, for he would have had to get through the Turkish lines, but I was told that an effort to trace them must be made and I took the next runner on the roster. I told him exactly what his job was like, but he made no comment. As I never expected to see him again, we went a short way together and then, as we were alone, we decided to shake hands. The position on a roster may be of vital importance, and I often turned to it with heaviness of heart.

When darkness fell, the fighting died away somewhat. Both sides were exhausted. It was that period when we should have been advancing through the beaten Turks to the hills, but actually the infantry were lying where they had dropped in their weariness. About nine o'clock the general called to me. We were still under the dune by the beach.

'D'you know the position of each battalion?' he asked. I told him that I only had a rough idea in the case of three battalions, while the other was, as I have explained, away somewhere on the northern hills.

The general looked old and haggard, worn out with worry and physical exhaustion. He had received the scantiest of information from the very beginning, and few definite orders, while the scheme of operations had gone badly astray. Reports from battalions constantly spoke of casualties of the senior officers and he had seen his colleague blown up with his staff. At the time he was talking to me the brigade major was up in front, and I was anxious about the orders I was likely to be given.

'I ought to be in touch with each battalion HQRS,' he muttered anxiously. I agreed, and told him that runners were getting through without much difficulty.

'What about your telephones?' he asked. 'I think you ought to run out a line to each of the battalion HQRS, at the very least.'

I told him of the small amount of wire we had saved

from the landing; of the difficulty of laying a line in the dark over unknown country, where there was no definite enemy line; and of the possibility that we might not find the vague map positions given.

The general stiffened in anger. 'You can at least use the wire you have got. I must have telephone communications with my outposts.'

And that was that! Probably the final orders that my section were likely to get!

'If you give me that order, sir, I will get on with it.' He looked at me with a trace of hesitation and then briefly told me to proceed.

I never expected to get back from such an expedition, for I had only the vaguest ideas where our outposts had got to. There had been no orderly line of attack, for often the flanks of a company or battalion would be in the air, and parties of the enemy were left in the rear. In other words our new little trip looked like a premature attempt to march on Constantinople! My operation orders for the landing were easy to this job, for then I had a screen of infantry, whilst now we would merely be walking into the blue.

I stirred up the section, which took some doing, for we had been fighting now for twenty hours and had not had any sleep for about forty. I gave the orders and we got out the stores. My acting sergeant was incredulous of the general's orders, but made no comment when I explained.

It was pitch dark, but comparatively peaceful. I suddenly longed for the brigade major: he would have understood. I gave the order to march – and in came the brigade major!

'Hallo, what's all this about?' he asked, as he saw my section with drums and all complete.

'The general's orders, sir: he wishes me to lay a line to each battalion HQRS.'

The brigade major gazed at me thoughtfully, and then turned on his heel to where the general was sitting under the sandbank. I remained where I stood in the background, but I heard a few words.

'... impossibility, sir ... quite certain that you'll have no signal section in the morning ...'

He returned to me at length. 'The general thinks you had better wait until the morning,' he said briefly.

# 7

## THE EIGHTH OF AUGUST[1]

By this morning the battle had already been lost. We did not know it, of course, but early failures and depressing reports from other fronts did not conduce to good spirits. In addition the state of affairs behind our lines was still bad. We now had a better supply of water and rations, but transport was in confusion – and considering the difficulties of the beaches, nothing else could be expected. The wounded were always in a pitiable state, especially in the earlier stages of the battle. Little could be done for them except to lay the cases on the beach, and relieve their pain. They lay in the heat of the sun, always under shellfire, short of water, or proper attention. The rate of mortality must have been nearly a hundred per cent on the first day, for gangrene set in so quickly. Parts of the battlefield were highly cultivated, so that if any wound became contaminated by the soil, it was almost a hopeless case. One heard of the gangrene spreading so quickly that limbs were operated on twice in one day, and a matter of an hour might make the difference to a man's life.

The medical service never worked so hard or devotedly, while the padres administered the last offices in the broiling sun for hours at a time, until they also dropped. It was reported that one good padre who had sailed over with us continued until he was nearly unconscious; and then became raving mad.

The British Army sprawling on the Suvla Plain was simply inert from lack of rest, or food and drink, and from depression. The best of its officers and NCOs, and about one-third of its number, had already been destroyed. A brave and resourceful enemy still stood unbeaten on the hills around. All ranks had been hard at work or battle since the dawn two days earlier and there had been no chance of anything more than a doze at odd times on the previous night.

It is true that a landing had been accomplished; that the first objectives had been gained; but these were mere preliminaries to the task which still remained.

The deadly inertia extended from corps to private soldier. The Staff, on that morning of the eighth, had but a vague idea of the position of their units. Divisions were intermingled, brigades were under the orders of other generals, and it was almost impossible to say even where a particular battalion headquarters was to be found. Having found it, one learned that companies were missing, that all senior officers were killed or wounded, that everyone was dead-beat. One could try to arouse the tired men, and they would drag themselves to their feet. And this was only the eighth! Where was the thrust to come from, which would take the army through to the Narrows?

Sir Ian Hamilton knew of the pressing urgency to

capture the heights before the Turks could bring up reinforcements, but the difficulty was to get anyone to move.
Corps Headquarters seemed satisfied with progress, and
talked of reorganization. Divisions had become mixed
up in command. Brigades were hopeless. General Sitwell
of my own brigade (the 34th) was terribly worn out – he
had never been equal to such a strain – and had become
entirely devitalized. He could not forget what his troops
had suffered by way of hunger, thirst, and – worst of
all – exhaustion. Even if orders had been issued at daybreak, it would have been a most difficult task to get
them to the units under his command, in the confusion
which existed on the front line.

It is said that on this morning the troops lay scattered
around as if in Hyde Park. Demoralization is suggested,
and that there were few casualties to warrant such a
state.

Once more one has to go back to fundamentals: to
the scourge of diarrhoea – now far worse; to the utterly
strange environment; to the psychological effect of the
horrors of the previous day on the minds of very raw
soldiers; to the loss of the best of the soldier-leaders;
and – above all – to the lack of anyone with the will to
*drive*.

I well remember that hot morning, and the lethargy
of hopelessness which brooded over everyone. We were
still not far from the shore, and my signal station was
functioning by means of runners. Any idea of a telephone was out of the question owing to shortage of wire
generally, as well as constant moves by the headquarters
of battalions.

It was at this time that Irish battalions of the 10th

Division arrived from their northern landing. They turned for an attack on the Chocolate Hill – but there was no support!

The RAMC must have a terrible story to tell. When they got their tents and personnel ashore their first difficulty was to find a suitable location for their stations. The beaches were the only places, yet they were under heavy and constant shellfire. The first one I visited had, a few minutes previously, lost two MOs and nearly half the staff from a shell which came straight through the roof of the tent. In fact the Turks sent a message objecting to the position of the hospital tents, and regretting the casualties, for the enemy was meticulously careful where hospitals were concerned. Apropos of this, we used to watch the desultory bombardment of the fleet, which would sometimes withdraw some distance from the shore. The huge hospital ship, however, rode within easy range of the Turkish gunners, and never moved whatever the gunfire, but she was left severely alone.

Later the wounded were taken off in the lighters, and although this story deals in everything which is ghastly I cannot tell you of the terrible scenes that ensued.

In the conditions which I have narrated we had to fight, and you can guess that many wild and fantastic stories were passed around. There were messages that some battalion was fighting with a flank entirely in the air, of some isolated company which was reduced to a few men under an NCO. Then again the Turks would make sporadic counter-attacks, and we would hear of our line being broken. The most terrible affair was the burning of the low scrub caused by the shellfire. Our men were hopelessly caught in it, and were simply burned to death, while the wounded lying out in front were gradually overwhelmed and no one could help. The clouds of smoke and rolling flames were an added horror, for we knew the infantry must be fighting through it. A complete company of the Norfolks[2] advanced to an attack and were never heard of again. They disappeared and were consumed, nor can the Turks, even now, give any adequate explanation. Not one man ever came back to tell us what had happened.

On this morning, the general decided to move brigade HQRS nearer to the front line, and I was ordered to lay a line from the beach to a spot indicated beyond the real Hill 10.

The beaches and ground behind the front through which I had to lay my line were comparatively quiet, for the enemy was concentrating his efforts in trying to beat back the attacks to the right of our position in the direction of Chocolate Hill. I had only covered about four hundred yards, when I saw a number of our troops streaming towards me. They did not belong to my brigade.

'What's the trouble?' I asked the leading man.

'Something's gone wrong back there', one of them replied with a jerk of his head to the firing-line beyond Chocolate Hill. 'We've got no officers, and no bloody orders, and the Turks are just coming through.'

A signal section is not likely to turn back some hundreds of men, and I knew they would soon be rounded up on the beach. I suppose I ought to have made the effort myself, but they looked pretty used up and I thought it was hopeless.

Cowardice is a subject which has received a good deal of attention in war books, but I doubt whether it deserves such interest. Nature seldom produces anything completely true to type, either physically or mentally, so that one man cannot be expected to display a particular emotion in conformity with its definition. Yet, on the other hand, all of us have something of every virtue or vice tucked away in our constitutional make-up. Hence cowardice is probably present in every man, and the degree to which it gets the upper hand depends not only on his other qualities which can master or mask it, but also upon the circumstances which weaken his mental strength. Sometimes one would meet the real coward, but he would be one of a crowd of normal men and often got through by clinging to their example or help. Generally he was, quite apart from his cowardice, of poor moral fibre or, still more likely, a neurasthenic. Apart from these few examples, the civilian soldier was sometimes brave and sometimes a coward and, still more often, exceedingly brave to hide his fear. If his cowardice got the upper hand it was generally because his nerve had given out; and it speaks a good deal for our armies that his symptoms were recognized as physical – and therefore medical – reactions which required definite treatment. It is true that, for sudden attacks of panic, drastic remedies were required; but this is obvious, since panic spreads so quickly. Firmness is essential in hysteria, which is of similar character to panic. I once was present on a parade in very hot weather, when men started fainting, and I was highly indignant when the officer in command roared out that the next man who fainted would go straight into the guardroom. But I forgot all about the idea of fainting, and so did everyone else!

Cowardice must be treated severely because of its contagious character, but otherwise it is a quality which every man had to fight himself. I had times of complete panic, and yet could be quite cool at others. I saw no sign of cowardice on the landing, but, after the troops had been worn out with thirst, heat, disappointment, and the loss of officers and comrades, their mental strength weakened with their physical endurance. Yet after rest such men would and did again recover their moral fibre. Colonel Kelly, who commanded a battalion in our brigade, tells of a man who displayed the most errant cowardice in Gallipoli and who, subsequently in France, was awarded the Victoria Cross.

By the way this subject has been harped on in plays and books, one would imagine that cowardice was unknown in civil life. I should have thought that 'guts' were just as much required now as fifteen years ago, and that many men who are in gaol for lapses of the law often require medical treatment rather than punishment. At any rate I hate the presentations of fictitious characters who were supposed to have fought through the war with an unvarying display of clear-cut emotions.

There was a great story of a battalion down Helles way, who were caught napping in a surprise attack by the Turks. They were just stirring in the early dawn when the Turks were on them; and they precipitately fled in complete panic. The enemy was held up by the reserves for a short time, and the battalion suddenly realized that they had really run away. Weapons of every description were seized and, in their 'night attire', which means that in some cases there were no trousers, the entire battalion counter-attacked with such ferocity that they not only swept the Turks away, but they also captured the first of the enemy trenches.

So when I saw a bunch of men coming back to the beach, and saw that there were no officers or NCOs there, I guessed they had been cut up pretty badly somewhere, but would be soon ashamed and wanting to get back.

In the meantime I was a little anxious in connection with my telephone line, for I was not keen on meeting the Turks in a victorious advance. However I was determined to show that we were not windy, and we carried on through the retreating infantry. Before we were clear of them they began to waver, and I heard afterwards that they were easily rounded up and sent back. I saw no sign of anything unusual ahead. Away to our right the battle for the heights beyond Chocolate Hill was still in fierce progress from two sides, the infantry attacking from our front and from the Anzac side as well. To our immediate front was the village of Anafarta, now almost demolished by the terrific bombardment from the fleet. It was about two miles away, and our new brigade HQRS was in that direction. We were skirting the left bank of the salt lake, which was entirely dry. On the original landing the advance had been ordered to go round the lake, since it was not known whether there was water or marshland there, but in fact it was hard, and later I often walked (or ran, when the Turkish gunners followed us with shells!) across its arid wastes.

On the hills the soil was rocky and dry, so that it seemed at times like sand, while low scrub was the only growth. Down the shallow valley in which we were laying our line the land was more fertile: fields appeared, both arable and pasture, and the scrub gave way to timber. Through these fields our attacks had been made on this front, the only cover being usually the hedges and ditches, although we did find some rough trenches which had been dug by the Turks some time ago, either for practice operations or for a real scheme for defending the bay.

Along these fields we laid our line, sometimes fixing the wire along the hedges or more often along the ground in the ditches. All the time there was a constant stream of men to and from the firing-line. Here was a party carrying up water, ammunition and rations; there a stretcher party taking back a gaunt figure swathed in blood-soaked bandages. Just slightly one could not help envying the wounded, for they would soon be snugly tucked away in the beautiful hospital ship down in the bay.

There were mules around by now, generally loaded up until their bellies sagged under the weight. My own section driver had been roped in for this service, and we used to see him trudging his phlegmatic way to and from the beach as I have already narrated.

The atmosphere was heavy with heat, dust, and decay. The acrid stench will remain in my nostrils forever. It had been my first impression on my visit to the Helles lines, and thereafter we were seldom out of it. Our dead were strewn over the whole battlefield, and often there were not sufficient reserves to provide burial parties. And just as gangrene attacked the wounded, so did decay set in for the dead.

I had to run a line for about a couple of miles, and I was hard put to find the length of cable. We only had what we carried ashore, and Divisional Signals was also short. At length we came to our reserve lines, and spent bullets began to whistle round our ears.

The brigade major decided to make brigade HQRS at a farm which had recently been captured, and we slowly worked our way there. Occasionally we would stop, put in an earth pin, and connect up to see if our line was intact, and communication was through to the oper-ator on the beach. We came to the neighbourhood of the farm and an extraordinary sight met our eyes. The farm had evidently been abandoned in extreme haste. A primitive plough had been abandoned in a furrow, while an overturned cart, with the shafts broken, had been obviously used as cover in the attack. We heard that the inmates had themselves fought, including the women, until they had been driven out or killed; and later, when we were vastly troubled with snipers, as you shall hear, it was generally believed that the occupants of the farm, including a girl, had secreted themselves behind our lines to wreak their vengeance on us.

How many times, when doing a job do you find that the material runs out shortly before the job is finished! A parcel is wrapped up and you have, with much trouble, found a bit of string; then you hold the paper together and wind the string round it – only to find that you want another six inches! That usually leads to a general hunt and considerable annoyance, in the style of the cartoons of Gluyas Williams.[3]

When I tried to run my telephone line up to the farm-house, I had the best example of this predicament I have ever experienced, for I ran out of wire some distance short of our objective. In my case there wasn't anything very funny about it. We were more or less in the open and without cover, the enemy's fire was heavy, and I had no chance of getting more cable. I sent back the linemen to pick up any slack in the line, and we made some short cuts, but still we could not get up to the cover of the walls of the farm buildings. Soon the general and brigade major had arrived, and the former still could not under-stand why I should be short of stores. With much labour we pulled the line to within fifty yards or so of the sta-bling, and there I had to fix up my portable telephone.

The next few hours were a nightmare. The field of fire was directed on to the farm buildings from the front and from the flanks, so that a constant stream of bullets whistled round the sides of the wall and outbuildings, and in the angle of these converging streams we had to carry on. The air was full of the crack of bullets which sang just clear of us, but many strays came through, and we had no protection from them. I wonder how many times I tugged at that line, hoping to get another yard or so nearer the safety of the wall! Even there, however, in such confused fighting, there was no security. I do not know how far ahead was our front line, but the battle swayed back and forwards so that at times we seemed to be almost in the thick of the fighting. We were attacking towards the west, but made very disappointing pro-gress and, as the day wore on, evening brought us to a standstill. To me it seemed that anything like a vigorous counter-attack by the enemy would completely break our thin line, for before the afternoon was over most of the reserves had been thrown in.

The general soon took a very serious view of the situation. It had become obvious that we could make no further headway; in fact the question soon became whether we could maintain our very precarious hold of the valley.

I believe that the Turk had his hands full with the attacks to our right without making any attack on us, and that he was content with merely holding us up. If so, he did his job remarkably well, for certainly the brigade staff were anticipating a counter-attack all day, and were exceedingly doubtful whether we could hold on.

The spirits of the troops were pretty good, considering events of the previous two days. It was a case where the spirit was willing but the flesh had weakened, and when exhaustion comes there is bound to be loss of morale. There had been little opportunity for sleep, for meals, or even for a smoke. The troops consequently were already dirty and haggard, and we could not get our minds away from wonderful thoughts of the meals we would choose, or of clear-running brooks into which we could plunge. In addition the casualties had been appalling, especially amongst the officers, so the matter of leadership was even more serious. In spite of these hardships, the thin line fought on with true Northern fortitude, and it never occurred to me that they would break except under pressure from overwhelming superiority.

There comes a time when Nature provides some kind of mental narcotic which numbs the finer emotions. I do not understand psychology sufficiently to be able to undertake any analysis of this state of mind, but I think

# Comrades in Arms

Every successful army depends heavily on morale, and in 1914 local loyalties were just as powerful as general patriotism, if not more so. Being true to friends, background and place of birth were prime motivations as, all over Britain, groups of young men volunteered together in so-called 'Pals' brigades. Irishmen who lived in Newcastle joined the Tyneside Irish. Railway workers formed their own Pals battalion. Youngsters with artistic talent joined the Artists' Rifles. Arthur Beecroft began military life in the University and Public Schools Brigade. Men who were short of inches but not of fighting spirit were formed in Bantams' Battalions. Officially a Bantam was supposed to be between 5 ft and 5 ft 3 in tall, but the minimum height requirement was not too rigidly enforced.

The advantages of this recruiting system were to be demonstrated all too soon in the trenches of northern France and on the beaches of Gallipoli. Orders were obeyed unflinchingly because men did not want to let their pals down. However, this concentration of 'pals' meant that when disaster struck, whole communities would be affected deeply, with entire factories, streets, villages and towns ripped apart by heavy losses.[4]

there is something of true philosophy in it, emanating admirable qualities of fortitude, or perhaps from religion. There is also resignation to the worst, when one can only cry *kismet!* Even a murderer can go to the scaffold with firm tread, just as a soldier can fix his bayonet to meet oncoming masses with a yell of defiance. I felt this resignation very strongly, for there was so little else to feel. It was no good being a coward, for one couldn't run away, and it felt better to get on with one's job than merely to shiver under a miserable hedge. The most ignoble feeling was the wish to be put out of it quickly. Once or twice I almost longed for a shell to come over *plonk* – and then for merciful oblivion. That is the kind of cowardice which leads a man to blow off his fingers, or to expose himself in the hope of a superficial wound. When discovered it must be severely punished, for it is a breach of the soldier's first duty of comradeship: to stand by his pals to the last.

My section was in a bad way, for casualties had been heavy. Not only were a third of the personnel already gone, but I had lost practically all my skilled telephonists. I had to keep a good man on the beach, for the station there was the only link between our section of the line and divisional HQRS. He received messages, therefore, from our divisional general, and we could get directly through to give our reports. All this applied when the line was intact, and I have no idea how many times that day it was broken. The cable was only laid roughly, as described, along hedges and ditches, and the troops coming up from the beach were constantly falling over it. More than once I received the ominous report that pieces had been cut out, apparently deliberately, and this suggested that spies or snipers (from whom we suffered so badly at all times) were busy. The shortage of wire made the situation all the more difficult.

Another skilled operator was now acting as corporal, and when I had completed my line to the farmhouse in the morning, I found I had no reliable telephonist left. There was nothing for it but to work the telephone myself. I was not sufficiently skilled to send by Morse, so had to keep the line clear enough for speaking – no easy matter under the conditions. The portable telephones issued to us were not a great success. Sometimes the instrument would work and sometimes it wouldn't. We used to curse it during training, but we simply blasphemed over it in Gallipoli. I remember on one occasion when an operator had spent precious minutes trying to fix the buzzer without success, while the line was waiting for a special message: he suddenly lost patience, picked up the instrument and, with a curse, hurled it over the hedge. We left it there! Ultimately we found one or two instruments which were fairly reliable, and there used to be a great rush to get them first.

The linemen put in great work. Night and day they would have to go out repeatedly to repair breaks, often under heavy fire, in constant danger from snipers who had marked down the cable line. It was my old friend Sapper Y who was always at my elbow, and he seemed always to be next on the roster.

'Line's busted again, sir!'

'Hallo, there!' I would shout. Once again our communication to the beach was cut off.

'I guess I know where the break'll be,' Sapper Y would remark confidently. 'I think I'd better get along right away.'

And off he would go, quite cheerfully and rather enjoying himself, quite apart from the fact that his beard was now thick black stubble!

It was extraordinary how one lost all sense of the duration of time. I might have been a few hours outside that farmhouse, or it may have been a whole day – I simply couldn't say. The incidents of that time are vivid, but time itself got lost. I was in a well-frequented spot, and heard the news – either gossip from passers-by or something more authentic through the phone from HQRS. Just in front were the farm stables, which had been utilized as a casualty clearing station, and the wounded were constantly passing, either the walking cases or on stretchers. For the whole of the day the MOs and staff were at work unceasingly.

Even in this phase of the battle general information was scanty. Few knew the scheme of operations: whether we were still supposed to be attacking on our sector, or whether the Turks had obtained a tactical advantage. There seemed to be very little information at the rear, also, for troops coming up never knew their destination, and carrying parties always seemed to be lost. I remember a mule driver coming up to me as I sprawled on the ground with my telephone. He was a Scotty, quite a lad, and he seemed bewildered. He had not the least idea where he was to go, and we discussed the matter together. Finally he saw another mule in the distance and walked off slowly, his phlegmatic animal beside him. I watched him, and suddenly saw his hands go to his face. He cried out, and dropped the leading rein. Turning, he ran back to me, and the blood was pouring through his fingers ... he reached my side and fell across my telephone. Poor Jocky, they hauled him away to the station, but I felt that it was back to his mother that he ought to have been going. Yet in a few minutes I had wiped the boy's blood off my tunic and was busy with the general. I suppose one can get used to any sort of beastliness.

As the day passed our position was getting still more serious. Casualties in the front line had to be replaced, and our reserves were dwindling fast, so that soon there would be no second line at all. Then if there came a real attack from the Turks ...

For a wonder my line was intact, and I got through direct to the division, and the divisional general was found. As I heard the two generals discussing the position it struck me as no mean feat to have a line nearly three miles long across a battlefield, through which a conversation could be held. It was also great luck, and I listened in the greatest trepidation, expecting every moment that the line would break. The general explained the position, and insisted that we must have reinforcements: that the line certainly could not attack and might not even hold in the face of any sort of attack; and that the infantry of his brigade were absolutely exhausted. He spoke with extreme urgency and there could be no doubt that he was thoroughly alarmed. If you had been sitting with me by that phone, with the air alive with the rush of bullets (the firing had increased in intensity), knowing that we had practically no more men to throw in, you would have felt as we did. No reinforcements could be sent up as it transpired, and we had to wait in hope that the Turks would not risk an attack. Meanwhile the battalions around us were being slowly forced back, the men so weary that they hardly knew what they were doing.

I was so obsessed with the scenes at hand that I had little thought of what was happening on other fronts. Away to the right, in the distance, the slopes beyond Chocolate Hill seemed to be ablaze, and the bombardment from the fleet was still throwing up huge masses of earth and rock on the hills. We saw on our left the advance of the 10th Division, with one of our own battalions operating alongside. At one point the advance was held up by a small strong point, a rough fort largely composed of sandbags. Word was sent to a battery, which proceeded to demolish the fortification.

When the burst of shellfire was over, we saw a crowd of tiny figures rushing round, and they were again building up their little fort. It was typical of the Turk – always a great fighter when defending his homeland. It was not until the heap had been levelled out for a second time that the Turks retired.

It is an incredible, but true, fact that there were practically no enemy forces on these northern slopes, the commander of the defence having withdrawn most of his infantry to the slopes of Chocolate Hill. Our final objective was the valley through the centre of the range of hills directly facing us, the village being in the centre view. If we could have pushed home the attack on those northern slopes instead of in the centre, we could have taken the position in the flank, and little more than two miles beyond was the huge ammunition dump upon which the whole Turkish Army depended. Alas! We knew nothing of that at the time, nor could such a tactical plan have even been considered. Yet now it seems so obvious! By the attacks at Anzac and on Chocolate Hill we had drawn down the Turks' effective forces, and we could have then worked completely round Kiretch Tepe Sirt. Such a threat would have affected the position of the Turkish Army throughout the entire peninsula, and if ... but there you are!

The battle died down somewhat at night. Before sunset the general decided that he did not care for my exposed position and we moved the signal station away from the farm to a small field, enclosed by a substantial hedge, the centre of which was distinguished by an enormous shell-hole probably made by one of our fourteen-inch guns. In a ditch under the hedge I felt that we should get a measure of security unknown so far that day.

It was just before sunset that I had my first experience of that unseen terror, the sniper. There was a row of us sitting along the bank under the hedge. Suddenly there came the crack of a shot, and a bullet came through the hedge and buried itself beside the foot of a major a few paces away from where I was sitting. From the angle of flight the bullet could not have come from the firing-line, and the sound of the shot had been remarkably close. Behind our field was a huge oak tree, rather a rarity on the usually barren peninsula. It was under this tree that I had been sitting the whole day, so when someone suggested that a sniper might be hidden in the tree I was frankly scornful. The excitement died down; and then, a few minutes later, 'crack' came the sound again, and this time the general himself nearly took one in the head. There was immediately a rush out of the field and troops fired volleys into the leafy shades of the tree. By this time it was getting dark, and there were conflicting statements of what transpired. Some said a sniper was shot out of the tree, but that he afterwards got up and ran off. I think it is possible that he fell out and got away – in any event it was not long before more bullets came whipping through the hedge, this time from a different angle.

A night of fitful sleep, in which we would spring up ready for instant action; occasional bursts of fire from the front; terrible weariness of mind – the fateful day of lost opportunities had gone.

# 8

## ON SNIPERS

It would be difficult to overestimate the effect of the efforts of the Turkish snipers. They caused considerable casualties, but the demoralizing result was far worse.

Imagine yourself leaving the front line for the beach. It often meant that you were exchanging comparative quietness for general discomfort; for there was nothing like so much heavy shelling of the forward infantry as there was of the beaches. You would slip away as quickly as possible, using hedges and ditches until you were out of range of ordinary rifle fire. Then perhaps you would come to the salt lake. If you were with a party it would be necessary to spread out, for the Turkish gunners were careful with their shells and would only risk a salvo if the target looked sufficiently tempting.

Just as you were thinking that you had dodged trouble – *crack!* – if you were lucky the shot fired at close range from some hidden spot missed you. But it would scare you as nothing else I can think of. Your sense of security was gone, and you would not be able to get out of your mind the fear that other lurking marksmen were watching your every movement. Every tree was suspect, every ditch dangerous. It got on your nerves as a basic kind of terror.

I have told already of two experiences with snipers; that of the fixed rifle at night, for this must have been some sniper within our lines, and the man in the tree who shot at us through the hedge. Very soon there grew up the most fantastic tales, most of them partially true but embellished by the imagination of the teller. There was one story of a woman who was supposed to be one of the inmates of the farmhouse. She figured in a dozen different versions. One was that she was found up a tree and, when killed, had a number of identity discs on her, representing the victims of her rifle. Another story, which I believe to be correct, was that one sniper was in a tree and was disguised as a branch, leaves being entwined in hair and clothing and the face browned to resemble bark.

I had considerable first-hand knowledge of these unpleasant gentry. Walking down to the beach one day, when I was quite two miles from our front line, I nearly took a bullet through the head. I tried to make out where the sniper was hiding, but had no luck at all. I guess they would change position very quickly, and there was any amount of suitable cover. Later on, other troops coming down the same path met with the same reception, but there was no agreement as to the hiding place.

Another remarkable episode was when I had fixed a signal station just east of the salt lake, in a shallow ravine. It was a peaceful spot, for we were sufficiently in rear of the infantry to avoid rifle fire, while there was no obvious target for the guns. At the time there was a lull in the fighting, and I had partially stripped in the hot sun, and had been dozing.

A sudden shout made me sit up quickly, and I saw a weird apparition standing a few feet away from me, gazing at us in surprise. He was festooned with leaves, and the features of his face were obliterated with paint. I was most interested in the rifle in his hand, and I leapt up to get my revolver from its holster. There were various other men in the ravine, who also seized their rifles. The Turk gave one quick look and then took to his heels, while we streamed after him in hot pursuit. My revolver was unloaded and useless, but we ran across a field and the Turk galloped away, cutting the most extraordinary capers to upset our aim. My RE corporal had a couple of shots but missed, and then others joined in, but everyone was so excited that the firing was only dangerous to ourselves. Our quarry plunged into some bushes, and we never saw him again!

The infantry seemed unable to cope with this sort of warfare, and that is not surprising, for they had had no experience of, or training in, stalking a hiding sniper, while the Turkish sniper was adept at open fighting, and probably knew the country. We suffered without retaliation until the division called in the aid of some Australians, who tackled the job thoroughly and systematically cleared up the country behind our lines. One could not but help admire the spirit of a man who would deliberately steal through an enemy's lines at nightfall, and then lurk in trees or scrub until he could find a victim. He knew that if he was captured, he stood a good chance of meeting the fate of a spy.

# A Dangerous Job

Turkish snipers were a constant source of concern for Arthur Beecroft and his fellow soldiers. The snipers were trained well by the German Army and highly accurate. Often they would hide near water-holes in an attempt to pick off unlucky Allied soldiers.

But the Allies, too, used snipers. Some – like William 'Billy' Sing from Queensland, Australia – became well known, and their tally fêted in the British and Australian press. An entry in an ANZAC war diary for 23 October 1915 states:

'Our premier sniper, Trooper Sing, 2nd L.H.,[1] yesterday accounted for his 199th Turk. Every one of this record is vouched for by an independent observer, frequently an officer who observes through a telescope.'

Each morning before dawn Sing would find somewhere suitable to hide and watch over the Turkish troops in their trenches. Sitting patiently with a 'spotter', he would wait for an enemy soldier to come into view. To avoid becoming a target of the Turkish snipers, he and his 'spotter' would often stay in their position until nightfall. It was a dangerous role and once Sing himself narrowly avoided becoming the target of sniper fire, with his 'spotter' taking the worst of it.

Of course, snipers were not the only foe at this time, particularly for troops like Arthur Beecroft. The difficult terrain and the constant heat could sap the energy and morale of even the most positive of soldiers. In his telling account, Arthur describes many of the privations suffered by him and his fellow soldiers, who each day had to contend with swarms of flies, dysentery, diarrhoea, thirst, and the prospect of death.

# 9

# THE NINTH AND TENTH[1]

The General Staff had at last decided that we required a stiffening of fresh troops on our sector.

Even from the front line we could see the activity on the sea and beaches, and we heard that a new division was to be landed and rushed up to the line.

At the time I was in a declivity behind the second line, with the reserves of one of our battalions. Officers, NCOs and men were in like condition of pitiable exhaustion. The state of the troops was not so desperate as in the earlier phases of the battle, notably as on the 7th August, but even ready supplies of rations and plenty of water cannot make up for lack of rest and the depressing effect of casualties. In respect of the latter, one could not help noticing how units had dwindled. One would see a group of men – perhaps less than a couple of platoons – holding some hedge and one would enquire from the company HQRS, only to find that the remnants of the whole company were there. It was quite the exception to find a field officer in the division at all, and companies might be commanded by junior captains or subalterns.

After the 7th August, our division had made little, if any, progress; on the contrary, on some sectors we had the greatest difficulty in holding the ground we had captured. The Turks had brought up reserves all along the line, with a great increase of firepower. When one went up to the firing-line one immediately realized this increase of enemy pressure. I know that it always seemed to me that any further advance was out of the question, and that at any moment the Turk might assume the offensive. If they had done so, against troops in such desperate condition as ours, there could have been only one result – we must have been simply swept away. The line was only thinly held, and the reserves were a mere handful.

I guess that my mental reactions at that time were a fair reflection of the majority. I had lost faith in the whole expedition, and my mind was bitter over the patent blunders which, from the very beginning, had marred our chances of success. Even if one has a real sense of discipline and loyalty, one cannot help realizing mistakes, especially if one is the victim of them, nor can free discussion be prevented. We thought that much of our suffering had been largely preventable. The errors over the landing, where units got lost and even fought each other; the confused scheme for the first attack; the chill of that first night without cover, followed by the heat of the day; appalling thirst such as few have been called upon to suffer; severe casualties and increasing disease – can it be wondered if we strained our eyes towards the beach, hoping for relief?

I was in a pretty bad way myself, for the gastric trouble had become acute. For the several days since the

landing I had not been able to manage to eat, and I suffered from continual pain. I had no energy left, my one
great desire being to sleep. It required a great effort of
the will to do the smallest job.

The Kitchener Divisions have been blamed for the
fiasco in Gallipoli, but I say that so far as the rank and
file, as well as the regimental officers are concerned,
such a criticism is quite unfounded. It may well be that
regular troops would have put up a better show, but that
comment is only a reflection on the training of Kitchener's New Army, not its spirit. I wonder what other troops
would have suffered as our infantry suffered in those
first four days, and still have been found fighting hard at
the end of that time, as my division was doing when we
were eagerly watching the beaches for signs of relief.

'There they come!' was the cry, as, far away in the
distance, we saw waves of men slowly advancing. Away
back on the beach the air was thick with the woolly
bursts from shrapnel. The Turkish guns had increased
to a roar. We could almost mark the place of disembarkation of the new division; almost trace the forward
movement as the advance began. Most of the avenues of
approach to the front line were entirely without cover,
and we knew only too well that the Turks had trained
their guns to certain spots with deadly accuracy. The
gunners had been in the habit of shelling even a small
party, to which the only response was to cut and run
for it. What would happen if solid masses of men were
slowly advanced through these danger zones in full
daylight, within about six thousand yards of the enemy
batteries?

Almost neglected in the front line, so that we could

watch the scene unmolested, we heard the roar from the guns on the Turkish hills, and heard and saw the shells bursting in that unprotected valley.

We had already tested the coming joy of relief; we had thought of a real meal; of the sea in which to wash our filthy bodies; perhaps of a shave and undisturbed sleep. Now we began to feel dreadful doubt. Once more something was going wrong. Had someone committed another appalling bloomer?

We began to gaze at each other, words unspoken but fear and doubt in our faces. We knew the time of dis-embarkation, and when the new troops should arrive. Already time was flying and not a man had put in an appearance. Meanwhile that infernal boom of the guns on the hills, and the crack of bursting shrapnel in our rear, continued with no sign of decrease.

At length we saw a line of infantry stumbling along towards our positions. Very slowly they were going, the line constantly disappearing as cover presented itself. I could see them rising to their feet and running forward a hundred yards or so, then dropping again.

There seemed very few of them – just a thin line. We had expected waves of eager comrades who would sweep through us to the positions beyond, ready to resume the battle – and to relieve us. What could this mere handful of men be expected to do?

A couple of junior officers dropped into our ravine. Just as soon as I saw their drawn and white faces, in which their eyes seemed glazed with horror, I knew that our worst fears had been realized.

'Where are we supposed to be going?' one of them exclaimed.

'What were your orders?' I asked.

The officer waved his arm vaguely to the front: 'We were told to come straight up to the front line.'

He was in a bad way, and I looked out to the troops who were now huddled up behind our positions. They seemed pitifully young, and it was plain that, as fighting men, they were finished. God knows what sort of hell they had been through, but there were stories of disembarkation in full view of the enemy – that could not be helped unless it was done during the night – of close formations on the salt lake, where the Turkish shells had played complete havoc, and of a two-mile advance, most of which was in the open, under a constant deluge of shrapnel. And all the time the officers and ranks had but the vaguest idea of the scheme of their advance (if any there was), and but little information of their immediate objectives.

'The front line is only about a couple of hundred yards ahead', I told the officer. 'Have you come to relieve us?'

He gazed at me foolishly, as if he did not understand. 'We've had bloody hell!' he muttered. 'They caught us in close formation.' He shuddered and then swore horribly. 'Relieve you!' He glanced out on the remnants of his command, as they sprawled in the ditches like already dead men, and rose to his feet unsteadily. 'Come on, there, Sergeant —! Get those men up. Now then, we've got to get up to the front line yet – these are only the reserves.'

Just as if the Turks had absolute knowledge of the progress of the advance, the gunfire had dropped, giving place to rifle and machine-guns. Until the remnants of the reinforcements had reached our positions we had been left in peace, but now the ground was being sprayed with bullets, so that it was almost impossible to raise one's head from what cover was available. In silence we watched the new troops as they rose for their final rush. A greater contrast to our men could not be imagined. My own brigade troops were blackened with the sun, with dirt, and often by congealed blood. There was an air of resignation and fortitude about these battle-scarred veterans of four days of fighting! Nothing worse than they had tasted could now be presented to them; they had no thought of death by now, but only perhaps of sleep and peace. And now the reliefs had come – fresh troops in beautifully clean uniforms, their faces yet to be tanned by the sun, their equipment looking stiff and unused.

Not a cheer was raised; barely a word exchanged. We watched dumbly as the men stumbled away.

Instinctively belts were tightened. We had been in the line for – how long? – and we were likely to stay there. This new division had faded away. The whys and the wherefores were not known then, and I do not know whether they are known now, but it was quite obvious to us, as that broken line of youngsters disappeared, that one of our new divisions could be counted out of the fight for good.

The day wore on. We heard little more of our relief, nor did I ever see the troops of the new division again as a fighting unit. They were spread over miles of the line; here a platoon – or the remnants of it – there a handful under an officer or NCO who had attached themselves to another battalion.

Our line was slowly pushed back, until reserves mingled with the others. It was the real example of the thin cordon which stood, very feebly but unbroken, between the Turk and the beaches. There was no support now, no one else to push in; and once again we waited for an enemy attack which would have crushed us at once.

It never came, which is exceedingly fortunate.

# 10

## OUT OF THE LINE

I have been wondering how to head this chapter. I thought of 'In Rest', or 'Reorganizing', but neither aptly describes a mere transition from the front lines of Gallipoli to the beaches, which is all the rest that any units could expect; while there is not much reorganization about the calling of the roll plus an extra ration of rum.

We were sent back to the beach, and the relief was great. We could bathe, loll under the dunes at our ease, and find touch once more with the outer world.

There were, however, snags.

The worst of the lot was when the roll was called, for we then knew both our total losses, and missed some of our pals of whom we had heard no word. Casualties amongst the officers had been appalling – something like eighty per cent of the number who went into action. Our brigade had practically no officers of field rank left. I think this was a result of the fact that we wore our badges of rank, and the Turk always had an easy field of fire, and was an excellent shot. He could mark down an officer without difficulty, and account for him first. There was also the fact that, in those first four days after the landing, all ranks were in fierce hand-to-hand combat with the enemy, so that officers of senior rank took the same chance as others. We had not learned the lesson of keeping badges of rank inconspicuous, as was subsequently the rule in France.

Amongst other ranks half our strength had disappeared, and the proportion of dead was very high owing to the difficulty in evacuating the wounded in the earlier and fiercer phases of the battle. Yet another reason for the big casualty list has been given by the Turkish commander, who stated that our troops, when advancing, ran forward at their full height, apparently having not been taught to crawl or crouch, and having little idea how to use natural cover. The Turks have expressed admiration for the manner of our assaults, but surprise at the recklessness of them, with horror at the ease with which they could shoot down so easy a target. This applied more particularly on the second phase of the battle, when the Turkish commander had withdrawn the remnants of his small force to Chocolate Hill and the slopes beyond, where he desperately stood at bay, expecting to be swept away in the first assault. Then came the delay, giving the enemy a chance to consolidate their positions. When the attack came, in more or less open formation, the Turks simply shot it away.

Meanwhile, as I have already said, the northern heights of Kiretch Tepe Sirt, on which we had nearly a whole division operating, were open for an almost unopposed advance, with victory awaiting us – so to speak – round the corner.

The first day in rest was great. We arrived in small sections; here a handful representing a company, there a small group under a corporal who were the remnants of a platoon. It was simply pathetic. On all sides one heard such questions as 'Where's Dick?'; 'Did T— get away in the hospital lighter?'

Our spirits were at a very low ebb that day, and the issue of rum – our first, by the way – was a heaven-sent joy. It was marvellous to see how the light returned to dull eyes, how men threw their shoulders back once more, simply as a result of some very excellent liquor. I could never again believe that there is not a proper place and time for liquor, or that an all-wise Providence has not intended us to use it when human effort can no longer control mind or body. It came just at that moment when we – for all the damnable reasons which could only descend on us at one and the same time: exhaustion, realization of total and particular losses, sense of failure – were down and out, and it saved the situation. By the time we had lost its fillip, men were already eating, reading, bathing, writing home, repairing their clothes – the hundred-and-one jobs which obliterate undue emotion and give the mechanism of the brain and body opportunity to recover.

I went around the various units to get the news, and the day was spent in swapping yarns. Everyone looked very used up, especially the more senior in years. I knew already that several of our commanders would be taking a trip back to England, but it has always seemed to me that an elderly man who failed in Gallipoli is not nearly to be so blamed as the home authorities for sending him out there. If ever a campaign called for youthful ideas and vigour, it was Gallipoli, and I would have thought it was patent, long before we actually landed, that lack of real leadership was going to be our undoing.

The beaches were not much rest in reality, for the Turk was always busy with his guns. We on the Suvla Bay side were not so badly off as troops down Helles way, for there the Turk could give them hell from the Asiatic shore, where they had some really heavy guns. Still, it was bad enough for us, and bathing in particular was distinctly risky, with the water occasionally spraying up with shrapnel. They had nasty stuff in their shells, too, and many curious objects were produced which were supposed to have come from them, including even rusty old safety-razor blades!

A large sack was sent ashore from some sportsmen in a cruiser for our mess. There were fresh vegetables, fruit and – greatest joy! – some Turkish cigarettes. I wish I could remember the name of the ship, for it was a real Good-Samaritan act which deserves personal thanks. Those cigarettes tasted better than anything I ever remembered.

After a few days rest we took over some reserve trenches, for the battlefield had settled down into opposing lines. On the second day in our new position the brigade major told me to go sick.

From the dusty soil of Suvla, with its pungent, acrid stink of explosives and decaying flesh, with its memories of desperate endeavour and failure; from the land of flies, lice and foul disease, hunger and thirst, I was taken to a cool and quiet hospital ship. As I snuggled down between the sweet-smelling sheets, in spite of my contentment, I felt that I had failed those few remnants of my division who still had to continue the hopeless fight.

A blurred and confused impression of a four-day battle, with its aftermath; a story of failure, yet of failure with a glory of its own. There are thousands of my friends and comrades lying buried in the arid soil of Gallipoli, and no soldier has laid down his life more worthily. If the few who ever read this short account can recapture the spirit in which that enterprise was undertaken by our civilian-soldier, they will find in it something as noble as any deeds of the war: the picture of the grim British Tommy just sticking it out until death found him.

# Journey's End

Lord Kitchener, at first reluctant to pull the exhausted Allied soldiers out of Gallipoli and so admit defeat, changed his mind after journeying to the peninsula and assessing the position for himself. The evacuation, which began with troops slipping away from Suvla and Anzac Cove and ended at Cape Helles in the early morning of 9 January 1916, turned out to be the only completely successful Allied operation of the entire campaign. It was meticulously planned and perfectly brought to conclusion.

Some 83,000 men were taken off the beaches and with them came 4,500 horses, mules and donkeys, 2,000 vehicles and 200 pieces of artillery. The withdrawal called for a peak performance by the men and officers of the Royal Engineers. They kept roads, jetties and piers in good order and crawled into no-man's-land by night to rig up wires, and lay mines that would discourage the Turks from becoming too inquisitive. The troops were withdrawn in stages and, as their ranks thinned out, ingenious tactics were employed to confuse the enemy. The guns were kept silent for long periods, so that once the silence became permanent it would take the Turks some time to realize what was happening. Rifles were rigged up to fire when increasing weights of water acted on cords attached to their triggers. The result was that an operation, which might well have been as costly as a major battle, was brought off without loss.

# AFTERWORD

## SOME PSYCHOLOGICAL
## ASPECTS OF WAR

A professional soldier is never likely to become introspective about his war experiences, for his earliest training is wholly directed to the control of the emotions. Nearly everyone knows fear, the most dangerous reaction in a soldier's mind, and consequently a recruit must be taught to overcome it. He is given discipline, *esprit de corps*, and a sense of comradeship, which will stand him in good stead when he gets the inevitable attack of 'cold feet'.

A good soldier will never deny fear, but he will certainly try not to show it. It is not a matter to be discussed, since he is deemed to be able to control it. Can one imagine any great fighting man of the past discussing his feelings with intimate details? What of Nelson lying on the deck of the *Victory*, or of Sir Richard Grenville in the face of the Spaniard fleet, or of the men who stormed the glacis of Sebastopol? We have many and varied accounts of those old battles, but the pages breathe self-sacrifice, ardent patriotism, and the joy in duty well and truly done:

> Sink me the ship, Master Gunner — sink her,
> split her in twain!
> Fall into the hands of God, not into the hands
> of Spain!

*The Revenge: A Ballad of the Fleet,*
Alfred Lord Tennyson

Fear sometimes became the subject for a play or novel, in the guise of cowardice. The two emotions are quite different, for fear is not ignoble, while cowardice represents lack or loss of control. In A.E.W. Mason's book *The Four Feathers*,[1] the hero is displayed as a bad soldier, because of his cowardice; and he obtains his salvation not by eliminating his fear, but by putting an iron control upon it.

It seems that the Great War has produced a type of writer who glories in dissection of the civilian-soldier's mind. Such writers tell battle stories from a new angle. As we are taken through the battlefields, our attention is drawn not to great feats of arms, but rather to the heaps of the slain. As we stumble (without camera, perhaps) after some young Cockney towards the German lines, with the barrage bursting round, and the machine-gun bullets ripping the air, we do not follow a train of thought in the soldier's mind of desire to capture the enemy trench, or glory to be won, or of possible death with face towards the enemy. No, we hear that he is blindly doing as he is told, that he has no hatred for the enemy he is told to kill, and that he knows how useless is the whole business of war. Then is the picture of stark fear presented to us: the chattering teeth, staring eyes, quivering limbs. Then come side-lights of the women waiting at home; so that misery is piled on misery.

The professional soldier could not write like that, for he would be presenting a man who had not fully learned the soldier's job, whose mental reactions had taken charge, thus weakening the will to face the task ahead. This is not to deny that many good soldiers have fits of cowardice, nor that heroes loathe war and long for the peace of home, but the weakness of the flesh has to be overcome, and a good soldier is not anxious to parade his weaknesses for the edification of any kind of public.

The civilian-soldier army of 1914–18, embracing all types, made its influence felt in different degrees. Many civilians became very good soldiers, while others, although carrying the insignia of the fighting man, never ceased to be civilians. Unfortunately, what we have so often is the autobiography of the man who had never become a soldier, the type who rather took pride in doing the necessary job, yet remaining aloof without appreciating the worth of the true fighting man's mind.

Such a man would now retort 'I had to fight, but I would never become a soldier. I always saw the horrors of battle, felt the misery. I could shoot down an enemy, but I could not forget it afterwards. I am glad that I always kept my sensitive feelings, and did not get brutalized by war.' That sounds all right, but it is nevertheless false. A soldier feels fear, lust, and the brutalizing effect of war; his soul reacts with sympathy, sorrow, or even stark horror; but any introspective analysis of his emotions is alien to his training and professional instincts.

It will be immediately argued that these characteristics of the professional soldier constitute that very type – the militaristic – which makes light of war even if it does not actually encourage it. Hence we have, in so many tales of the war, ever recurring hatred of the 'brass-hats', not merely on the grounds of incompetence (which might sometimes be justified), but because of their supposed callous disregard for the sufferings of the common soldiers. So also are the present government keeping our fighting organizations as far in the public background as possible. Cadet Corps are denied financial support, and the annual pageants are being shorn of their military splendour. All this on the basis that there must be nothing in the present to make for the 'glamour' of war in the future.

It never seems to occur to these present-day pacifists that the training for a future war is precisely the same as that required to face for peace. In war there is much of fear, of hatred and of horror; and for each of these bogies of war the soldier is given a healthy corrective. When he is standing shoulder to shoulder with his mates he feels far less fear – thus learning the value of comradeship. He finds that discipline need not be irksome, and is a necessity. He discovers self-respect.

Surely every one of the horrors of war finds its counterpart in peace? Not so apparent, perhaps, but just as menacing. Have we not fear constantly at our side: fear for the future means by which to live, fear for our children, possibly fear of disease and suffering? Such fear can become cowardice, and ruin our characters with as dire results as if we had run away from a battlefield. Just so is there need for comradeship in peace as in war;

so that I sometimes think that if we had stood together during the last ten years as we did during the war there would have been a happier country than there is today. Go to a meeting of the British Legion and see what the old comradeship was like, or see the work of Toc H.;[2] for it cannot be gainsaid that the war produced a brotherliness between all classes which we never saw before, and may never see again. '*With our backs to the wall* ...'[3] and still able to stick it out! Don't we just want that same spirit now, whether we are facing the bad times in our family life, or the trouble of our country!

Of the terrible sufferings of the war, the broken hearts and maimed bodies, we find corresponding reflections also in these times of peace, except that there are no casualty lists, no burial with military honours, and few rewards for services rendered. We live in a curious world and Nature has dished up a curiously flavoured sauce for us, so that we require a strong digestion; hence perhaps the derivation of the word '*guts*', a wholesome attribute most certainly evident in our civilian armies during the war, but neither so obvious nor so admired at the present time. The fact is that war produces the virility in man, and woman acquires something of the same quality. In the path of the war comes the aftermath of broken manhood, with lessened vitality and willpower, resulting in loss of virility, so that it is reflected not only in the men who served, but in those who lived during that period, suffering mentally or physically during those years from nerve-strain and bad food. Perhaps it will be found that the women have retained that quality of '*virility*' which they acquired in the war period, for at the moment, in every walk of life, woman is showing the way for man.

The moral is surely obvious: that the war produced sterling qualities necessary to face the beastliness of it all; but that those same qualities are just as necessary in order to face the difficulties and dangers of the present time. Yes, I agree, stop all war forever! Let brotherly love rule the world. But see to it that the qualities produced by striving for a noble object can still be inculcated into men's minds; for otherwise there will come demoralization and degeneracy. If the training of our youth in arms is to be derided or abandoned, see to it that some other system takes its place, which can teach the same lessons of discipline, self-respect, and comradeship.

## The Reckoning

The toll of men killed or wounded in the Gallipoli campaign makes grim reading. Some 480,000 Allied soldiers were shipped to fight in the peninsula, and many of them never came back. More than 26,000 British troops died in battle; the Anzacs lost more than 10,000, the French some 8,000 and India more than 1,500. The number of men wounded was almost twice as high as that of men killed and, as seemed inevitable given the swarms of flies and a lack of adequate medical resources at Gallipoli, the number of those who succumbed to disease was greater than that of those killed by bullets and shells. There are no reliable figures for Turkish casualties, but they have been estimated at 65,000 killed and some 235,000 wounded.

It was not only lives that were lost. Reputations were

at stake too. Winston Churchill, most prominent and most enthusiastic of those who supported the venture, lost his job as First Lord of the Admiralty and bore the stain of his impetuosity until, in World War II, he was called upon to save Britain. General Hamilton, dismissed from command of the entire operation, had nothing to do afterwards than to write his memoirs. General Stopford, who failed to show any flicker of an aggressive spirit at Suvla, never held active command again.

An Australian journalist, Keith Murdoch, found a way through a labyrinthine system of censorship to expose the shortcomings of the generals. 'The continuous and ghastly bungling over the Dardanelles enterprise was to be expected from such a General Staff as the British Army possesses', he wrote. 'The conceit and self-complacency of the red feather men are equalled only by their incapacity.'

To set against a sorry tale of death and defeats, moments of individual heroism left an imperishable memory, and the performance under fire of the Anzacs helped to forge a new sense of nationhood. Australians in particular abandoned deference to the 'mother country' when they contrasted the performance of their own men with that of high-ranking British officers. Anzac Day, in remembrance of the landing on 25 April, 1915, is kept with special reverence.

# ENDNOTES

## An Apology

1. The Kellogg Pact (also known as the 'Kellogg–Briand Pact') was a multilateral treaty signed in Paris on 27 August 1928 by fifteen countries, including France, Germany and the USA. It came into effect in July 1929 with signatories having agreed to renounce war as an instrument of national policy and to settle all international disputes by peaceful means.

## Chapter 1 – Training

1. Beecroft is referring to the Franco-Prussian War of 1870–1, which resulted in France ceding parts of the provinces of Alsace and Lorraine to Prussia.

## Chapter 2 – With the Division

1. Beecroft means that it was odds-on that the general would speak into the wrong end of the telephone, i.e. that the general was not technologically minded.

## Chapter 3 – To an Unknown Destination

1. The reference here is to the ss *River Clyde*, which was a collier ship that had been requisitioned by the Royal Navy and adapted for use at Gallipoli. She took part in the landings at Cape Helles in April 1915 and was beached at V beach, where she was used as a quay and breakwater and a field-dressing station.

2. Beecroft means 'by their objectives'.

3. Beecroft's ancestor had fought at the siege of Acre on the side of the Turks

against the French. The siege began in late March 1799 when the forces of Napoleon Bonaparte sought to take the city, then under the control of the Ottoman governor, Ahmed al-Jezzar. Commodore Sir Sidney Smith, RN, came to the aid of al-Jezzar, helping him to shore up the city's defences. After a final bombardment in May, Napoleon gave up and withdrew his forces. His failure to take Acre was a turning-point in his bid to conquer Egypt and the East.

## Chapter 4 – Final Preparations

1. 'Water will be found on the mainland' forms part of Beecroft's orders for the invasion of Suvla Bay.

2. 'Hill 10' was the Allied name given to a low isolated mound to the north of Salt Lake and not far from the coast. Hill 10 was taken by the 9th Lancashire Fusiliers and the 11th Manchesters early on the morning of 7 August 1915.

3. Harry Tate and Will Evans were both popular comedians who specialized in farce before and after the First World War.

## Chapter 6 – The Dawn

1. 'Chocolate Hill' was the Allied name given to one of the hills to the east of Salt Lake; next to Chocolate Hill was 'Green Hill', and behind Green Hill was 'Scimitar Hill'.

## Chapter 7 – The Eighth of August

1. The year here is, of course, 1915.

2. The 'Norfolks' mentioned here are the 1/5th Norfolk Brigade, partly formed by many workers from the Royal Estate at Sandringham. Their mysterious disappearance during the heat of battle on 12 August 1915 led many to speculate what had happened to them on that fateful day.

3. Gluyas Williams was an American satirist and cartoonist of the first half of the twentieth century.

4. The practice of signing up new recruits into 'pals battalions' came to an end with the introduction of conscription in January 1916.

## Chapter 8 – On Snipers

1.   William 'Billy' Sing was a member of the Light Horse (LH) regiment.


## Chaper 9 – The Ninth and Tenth

1.   The events in this chapter occurred on 9–10 August 1915


## Afterword: Some Psychological Aspects of War

1.   *The Four Feathers* by A.E.W. Mason was a popular adventure novel, published at the beginning of the twentieth century.

2.   Toc H. is an international movement that was set up after the First World War to perpetuate the fellowship developed at Talbot House, a soldiers' club founded near Ypres in 1915. The name Toc H. comes from the phonetic alphabet used by Allied soldiers at the time. For further details, see www. toch-uk.org.uk.

3.   This quotation comes from Haig's Special Order of the Day, dated 11 April 1918. In his message to the troops, Field-Marshal Sir Douglas Haig urged all Allied soldiers in France and Flanders to fight to the very end:

> "… There is no other course open to us but to fight it out. Every position must be held to the last man: there must be no retirement. With our backs to the wall and believing in the justice of our cause, each one of us must fight on to the end. The safety of our homes and the Freedom of mankind alike depend upon the conduct of each one of us at this critical moment."

# TIMELINE OF KEY EVENTS OF THE GALLIPOLI CAMPAIGN

## 1914

3 Nov   For 10 minutes only, Royal Navy warships bombard the outer Turkish forts that guard the entrance to the Dardanelles

## 1915

13 Jan   British War Council approve plans for a naval attack on the Dardanelles

19 Feb   The Allied naval bombardment of the Straits' forts

23 Feb   Island of Lemnos (Mudros Bay) becomes the base for the Allied fleet

11 Mar   General Sir Ian Hamilton is appointed as Commander-in-Chief of the Mediterranean Expeditionary Force

18 Mar   Major naval attempt to force the Straits carried out during daylight by sixteen British and French battleships; attempt fails at the cost of losing three battleships, with three further ships disabled

25 Apr   Landings at Anzac Cove by the Australians and New Zealanders, and at Cape Helles by the British

28 Apr   First Battle of Krithia

6-8 May  Second Battle of Krithia

24 May   A 'suspension of arms' agreed so that both sides might bury their dead

| 4 Jun | Third Battle of Krithia |
| 28 Jun | Battle of Gully Ravine |
| 12–13 Jul | British forces attack Helles |
| 6–7 Aug | British attack at Cape Helles; Australians attack at Lone Pine |
| 7 Aug | 9th British Corps land at Suvla Bay before dawn |
| 15 Aug | Stopford is dismissed from command |
| 21 Aug | Battle of Scimitar Hill |
| 16 Oct | Telegram from Lord Kitchener recalling Sir Ian Hamilton |
| 27 Oct | General Sir Charles Monro takes over command of Mediterranean Expeditionary Force |
| 11 Nov | Winston Churchill resigns as Lord of the Admiralty |
| 8 Dec | General Monro orders Birdwood to proceed with the evacuation of Anzac Cove and Suvla Bay |
| 19–20 Dec | Allies evacuate Suvla Bay and Anzac Cove |

# 1916

| 8–9 Jan | Allies evacuate Helles |

# MAJOR PLAYERS

'What I want to say to you now very seriously is that the continuous and ghastly bungling over the Dardanelles enterprise was to be expected from such a General Staff as the British Army possesses, so far as I have seen it. The conceit and complacency of the red feather men are equalled only by their incapacity.'

*Australian journalist Keith Murdoch in a letter,*
*dated 23 September 1915, to Lloyd George*

*The biographical notes that follow are provided by Robin Hosie*

## Lord Kitchener (1850–1916)

When Great Britain declared war on Kaiser Wilhelm's Germany, the outstanding choice as War Minister – official title 'Secretary of State for War' – was Horatio Herbert Kitchener, recently ennobled as Lord Kitchener of Khartoum. His record in colonial wars was one of unbroken success. Leading an Anglo-Egyptian army at the battle of Omdurman in 1898, he had inflicted a crushing defeat on the fanatically brave but poorly armed followers of a Muslim religious leader known as the Mahdi. As well as restoring control of the vast Sudan to Great Britain, this healed a thirteen-year wound to British pride:

the death, at Mahdist hands, of the much-revered General Gordon.

Kitchener's contribution in the Second Anglo-Boer War was of even greater importance, for he brought it to an end. Outnumbered and defeated in major battles, the Boers had turned to guerrilla tactics and their hit-and-run commando attacks were inflicting severe damage.

By stationing troops in blockhouses and stretching hundreds of miles of barbed wire across the veldt, Kitchener put a brake on the Boers' most telling weapon – rapidity of movement. Then he cut off their sources of food and other supplies, by burning crops and imprisoning their families in what were termed refugee camps but amounted to concentration camps. The possibility that disease might flourish in such places seems not to have been considered, with the inevitable result that insanitary conditions ran rife. An estimated 25,000 Boer women and children were to die in the camps. Sir Campbell-Bannerman, leader of the Liberal Party, denounced 'the methods of barbarism' but back in Britain Kitchener's popularity was barely dented.

In August 1914, Kitchener realized that, contrary to the predictions of the armchair generals, the troops would not be home by Christmas. He expected a long war and his drive, typified by his 'Your country needs YOU' poster, created a vast volunteer army that saw the country through perilous times and put it on the road to final victory. He must, however, bear a heavy load of responsibility for the failures at Gallipoli. He was firmly against diverting men or experienced officers from the trenches in France so initially he agreed – and even that reluctantly – to an attack through the Dardanelles, but only if it was carried out by ships alone. When the naval attack failed he underwent a change of mind and decided that the army should move in. An admission of defeat, he believed, would have a very serious effect on British prestige in the East. Kitchener approved the landings at Cape Helles, Anzac Bay and later at Suvla. But he underestimated the fighting qualities of the Turks, and the generals he chose were drawn chiefly from the ranks of those who could best be spared. At least he had no hesitation in sacking those

who failed – men like Stopford and Hamilton. His most positive contribution to the Gallipoli venture came when he gave the order to
bring it to an end.

Kitchener was always reluctant to explain his decisions and
by 1916 even his admirers were beginning to question his style
of running the war as a 'one-man show'. There was relief in many
quarters when, on 5 June, he left the country on a mission to Russia.
But the nation was plunged into mourning when the news came
through that his ship, HMS *Hampshire*, had been sent to the bottom
by a German mine and, along with most of its crew, he had drowned.
Margot Asquith, wife of the Prime Minister, had a final unkind word:
'If Kitchener was not a great man, he was, at least, a great poster.'

# General Sir Ian Hamilton (1853–1947)

If victory in warfare went exclusively to those who behaved like gentlemen at all times, then Sir Ian Standish Monteith Hamilton, who
wrote poetry in his spare time, might have been remembered as a
great commander. He came from a military family and early in his
career he saw action in Afghanistan, Burma and both Boer Wars.
Twice he was recommended for the Victoria Cross but it was refused
on both occasions – the first because he was regarded as too young,
the second because he was by then too high in rank. It would have
been some consolation that he became Lord Kitchener's Chief of
Staff and won a knighthood.

When Kitchener asked him to lead some 70,000 men in the
attack on Gallipoli, Hamilton knew this was not enough, but he did
not insist on having this number increased. Preparations began but
there was no sense of urgency at Hamilton's headquarters and pro-
posed jumping-off point, the Greek island of Lemnos. Delay gave the
Turks time to treble their numbers in the peninsula to 85,000 men.

Hamilton, who started by underestimating the fighting qualities
of the Turks, had no idea of their numbers or positions and made
no serious attempt to find out. He had no up-to-date landing craft

and not even any reliable maps of the peninsula. Nor had the bulk of his troops been in action before. To add to these drawbacks, he was too much of a gentleman to overrule his subordinates and he found it hard to dismiss those who were incompetent. When General Hunter-Weston, leading the Cape Helles attack, was fought to a standstill outside the crucial village of Krithia, Hamilton suggested a night attack. Hunter-Weston refused, protesting that his men were not trained for night-fighting. Typically, Hamilton did not insist. And Krithia remained untaken.

Suvla Bay was Hamilton's last throw but even though the initial Turkish defence could summon up only some 1,500 men against twenty-two battalions, it too ended in failure. On 15 August 1915, Hamilton finally sacked the hopelessly incompetent Sir John Stopford. But this was on the orders of Lord Kitchener and was, in any case, too late. Hamilton's own sacking followed swiftly: after a long tale of disasters, he asked for more men. Kitchener's response, on 15 October, was to send him home.

With his military career over, Hamilton settled down to write his memoirs. He also worked tirelessly for the British Legion, becoming President of its Scottish branch. In a praiseworthy bid to turn former enemies into friends, Hamilton became a founder member and Vice-President of an Anglo-German Association in 1928. Such a forgiving posture could be carried too far. In the 1930s Hamilton, who had no great success as a general, made the greatest mistake of his life. He was naïve enough to welcome the rise to power of Adolf Hitler.

# General Sir William Riddell Birdwood (1865–1951)

It seems not to have occurred to Lord Kitchener that the men who came forward from Australia and New Zealand to fight for Britain in her hour of need should be led by an Australian or a New Zealander. But he did the next best thing: he gave command of the

Anzac Corps to a British officer who was to emerge from Gallipoli with his reputation enhanced rather than diminished. Sir William Riddell Birdwood, made a lieutenant-general when Kitchener put him in charge of the Anzac Corps, came to the responsibility with an impressive record. The colonial wars and skirmishes fought in the closing decades of the Victorian era had given young officers a chance to show their mettle, and Birdwood, after seeing action with the Bengal Lancers on India's ever-simmering North-West frontier, had served on Kitchener's Staff in the Boer War.

When Birdwood took command, the Australians and New Zealanders were in Egypt, training to fight in France. They were diverted to Gallipoli following the humiliating failure, in March 1915, of a naval attempt to force a way through the Dardanelles and threaten Constantinople. When the army was called in, the objectives of the Allies remained the same: to get warships through the straits, overawe the Turks with a threat to their capital and possibly drive them to sue for peace. To do this, the British and their Allies needed first to capture the high ground of the Kilid Bahr plateau. Then, it was expected, Turkish forts and batteries along the Narrows could be shelled into surrender or smithereens.

These high hopes came to nothing. At Anzac Cove, as at Cape Helles and Suvla, energetic Turkish commanders brought up reinforcements that tilted the balance against the attacking troops. At least at Anzac Cove the outcome was a close-run thing. Fighting in an unfamiliar terrain of jagged hills, precipitous gullies and near-impenetrable undergrowth, the Anzacs made some ground on the first day of fighting but were unable to hold it against reinforcements brought up by the dynamic Turkish commander Mustafa Kemal. They were forced to dig in on little more than a cliffside beachhead, under constant barrage by Turkish guns.

Birdwood, in charge of an attack that became a defence, won the admiration of the Anzac fighting men. He disagreed with the decision to abandon Gallipoli because he knew it would damage British prestige in the East, but he played an important part in organizing the only successful part of the entire enterprise – the evacuation. His performance in the peninsula led to command on the Western Front in France, where promotion came rapidly. He was in charge of an Anzac Corps at the Battle of the Somme in June 1916. In 1917 he was made a full general and in May of the following year he was given command of the British 5th Army in France.

With the war over, Birdwood was heaped with more honours: a baronetcy in 1919; a triumphant tour of Australia in 1920; Field Marshal and Commander of the British Army in India, 1925–30; Master of Peterhouse College, Cambridge 1931–38; a seat in the House of Lords as Baron Birdwood in 1938. He narrowly failed to become Australia's Governor-General, but his performance at Gallipoli came to be remembered in a more important and very human way: scores of towns, streets, roads, closes and avenues in Australia and New Zealand carry the name Birdwood to this day.

# Lieutenant-General Sir Aylmer Hunter-Weston (1864–1940)

In May 1916, Lieutenant-General Aylmer Hunter-Weston was honoured for his leadership in battle with a knighthood. Clearly, the rank-and-file soldiers who had the misfortune to serve under him at Gallipoli were not consulted. Hunter-Weston's grasp of infantry tactics did not go far beyond a fondness for full frontal assaults, as if the machine-gun had never been invented. In a metaphor drawn from the hunting field he called this 'blooding the pups'.

An eye-witness, John Churchill, wrote: 'These continual frontal attacks are terrible, and I fear the Generals will be called butchers by the troops. HW already has that name.'

There was never any doubt about Hunter-Weston's personal courage. He had proved it in India on the North-West frontier. In South Africa, Hunter-Weston (then, like Arthur Beecroft later on, an officer in the Royal Engineers), somehow managed to form an engineers' cavalry unit, which he led in daring raids on the Boers' railway communications. In 1914 he commanded an infantry brigade in France and the following year, despite Lord Kitchener's reluctance to take experienced officers away from the Western Front, he was put in charge of Britain's 29th Division for the 25 April attack on Cape Helles.

Sir Ian Hamilton, in command of the entire Gallipoli campaign, called him 'a slashing man of action'. There was plenty of action and more than plenty of blood at Cape Helles and in three savage battles for the village of Krithia, but very little in the way of success. On 29 August, Hunter-Weston was invalided home with what was called 'sunstroke', though whether or not that was the real reason has never been established. On recovering health, Hunter-Weston returned to France, where he commanded 8th Corps at the disastrous Battle of the Somme. Their casualties on the first day of the battle were 14,581 killed or wounded, yet they took only a handful of isolated German front-line positions that were all abandoned within twenty-four hours.

That was effectively the end of his military career. Given home leave in October, Hunter-Weston turned to politics, becoming MP for a Scottish constituency. He retired from Parliament in 1935 and died in 1940 after falling from a turret at his ancestral home in Hunterston. Perhaps the most perceptive comment on him as military leader was that of Field Marshal Haig, Commander-in-Chief of British forces on the Western Front, 1915-18: 'A rank amateur.'

# Sir Frederick Stopford (1854–1929)

In the springtime of his military life, Frederick Stopford cut a dashing figure. He was more than once mentioned in despatches for gallant deeds on behalf of Queen and Country in various colonial skirmishes and in the Anglo-Boer Wars. But as he advanced in years he became more and more cautious. His actions, or rather inaction, at Suvla came to represent all that was most humiliating about the performance of many Allied commanders at Gallipoli.

Birth and breeding combined to make Stopford the ideal choice when pomp and ceremony were called for. The son of an Irish Earl, he was chosen while a boy at Eton to be a page of honour to Queen Victoria. On the parade ground or in his capacity as the heavily be-medalled Lieutenant of the Tower of London, Stopford was an imposing figure. But he had never commanded in battle and when, at the age of 61, he was expected to take charge of flinging back Turks, he was less likely to shine. He got the job only because he was high on the army's seniority list and Lord Kitchener refused to spare a single experienced officer from the mud and blood of Flanders and France, where he knew that the war could be won or lost.

Stopford was given five fresh divisions for the Suvla Bay operation and the objective of taking pressure off the Anzacs and so giving them a good chance to take the high ground around Sari Bair. The Turks had no more than 1,500 men within five miles of Suvla but Stopford decided, without proper reconnaissance, that they must be 'heavily entrenched'. Instead of ordering a swift attack on the Tekke Tepe ridge, a few miles inland, he saw his most pressing duty as being to ensure that all stores were properly landed. He was indeed short of artillery and of water supplies, but these were matters that should have been resolved at the planning stage. While Stopford stayed aboard his sloop, with the unwarlike name of HMS *Jonquil*, the men on shore waited for orders that never came. Some took the opportunity to splash about in the sea. A handful had encountered the Turks but had turned back to the beach because of agonizing thirst. An astonished German officer recorded in his diary: 'It looked like a Boy Scouts' picnic.' Even Hamilton was moved to criticize Stopford's leadership and on 15 August, with the comment that Gallipoli was 'a young man's war', Kitchener sacked him.

For a couple of years he slipped back easily into his old ceremonial post at the Tower of London. He retired from the army in 1922 and was awarded a KCB, his second knighthood, though the justification for it must have puzzled the men he was supposed to have led at Suvla.

# Major-General Sir Frederick Hammersley (1858–1924)

Eton … Sandhurst … fighting dervishes in the Sudan with Kitchener … up against hard-feuding Boers in South Africa … the military credentials of Sir Frederick Hammersley looked to be beyond reproach. Yet it was both unwise and unfair of the War Office to bring him out of retirement and pitch him into the maelstrom of Gallipoli. It was even more unfair on the men of 11th Division, who were under his command at Suvla. For Hammersley had suffered a nervous breakdown just before war broke out, and had spent some time in a private mental home.

Assigned to capture a number of what were thought to be Turkish strongholds in the path of 11th Division, Hammersley was no more an enthusiast for taking the offensive than his immediate superior, General Stopford. And Stopford seemed more concerned with landing supplies than with using them against the enemy. When Hill 10, a key prominence overlooking Suvla Bay was finally captured, it turned out to have been defended against some 3,000 British troops, by a little over one hundred Turks. Hammersley stayed rooted on the hill, sending out orders, then contradicting them. General Hamilton, in charge of the entire Gallipoli operation, urged him to make a swift advance, but Hammersley argued that this would mean a costly night attack, with no certainty of success, and Hamilton gave way.

This gave the Turks plenty of time to bring up reinforcements. At the height of the confusion Hammersley had a second nervous collapse that led to his being relieved of command and invalided home.

There was no lack of reasons and excuses for his performance at Suvla. Many of his men were suffering badly with dysentery, they were short of food, water and ammunition, and nobody had any idea how many Turks they were facing. But generals are meant to overcome obstacles and Hammersley's innate caution overwhelmed any offensive spirit he may have demonstrated in earlier years.

# Kemal Ataturk (1881–1938)

Even as a schoolboy, Mustafa Kemal, the founder of modern Turkey, stood out from the crowd. The name Kemal, bestowed by his teachers, means 'the perfect one'. After this promising start it was at Gallipoli that he began to emerge as a man of destiny. In command of the Turkish 19th Division at the time of the Anzacs landing, he was astonished and angered at the sight of some Turks running away. When they excused themselves by pointing out that they had run out of ammunition his response was: 'You have your bayonets.' He made them lie down, halting the advance and giving the order for reinforcements to arrive at the double. It did his reputation no harm when, at a later engagement, a watch carried in his breast pocket saved him from harm when shrapnel struck him on the chest.

Before the war, Kemal had shared many of the aims of a group of army officers known as the Young Turks, who were set on a radical modernization of Turkish society and bringing an end to corruption. They lost influence after 1918 and it was left to Kemal to lead resistance to a peace settlement, dictated by the Allies, that gave large swathes of Turkish territory to Greece. He led a nationalist rebellion, expelled the Greeks and, in 1922, brought the centuries-old despotic rule of the Ottoman sultans to an end. Turkey was declared a republic the following year and Kemal became its first President.

He set about modernizing the country with an iron hand. And that meant Westernizing it. Islamic law was swept away, to be replaced by a system of law based on European codes. Women were given the right to vote. Arabic script was rejected in favour of the Western alphabet. Educational reforms included a nationwide literacy campaign. Kemal even prohibited the traditional Turkish headgear, the fez. He introduced the use of surnames, and it was only fitting that the one allotted to him was Ataturk – 'Father of the Turks'.

# Liman von Sanders (1855–1929)

The Ottoman Empire, once the scourge of Europe, began to slide into a long decline after 1529, when its army was turned back from the gates of Vienna. By the nineteenth century, Turkey was 'the sick man of Europe' – a byword for corruption, debt and random cruelty. The Sultan, Abdul Hamid II, began to cast envious eyes on German efficiency. He was deposed in 1909 by the Young Turks (see *Kemal Ataturk*), a group of revolutionary officers who shared at least one idea with him: that Turkey was in dire need of German advisers.

It was against this background that, in December 1913, Liman von Sanders was appointed to lead a German military charged with bringing new life, discipline and efficiency into the Turkish Army. By August 1914, he was in command of the Turkish 5th Army in Gallipoli. He took skirmishing by warships at the mouth of the Dardanelles in February 1915, as a warning of British intentions and rushed to build up Turkish forces in the peninsula. Unlike many of his counterparts among the British generals, he was ruthless in dismissing officers who showed incompetence. By the time of the Allied landings on 25 April, he had six divisions – 84,000 troops – waiting for them. He made a mistake in forecasting where the Allied forces would attack, and this accounts for so many of the landing beaches being poorly defended. But that was only at first. He was masterly at bringing up reinforcements, and the landing places at Helles, Anzac Bay and Suvla were turned into little more than gallantly defended beach-heads. Appointing Mustafa Kemal to repel the Anzacs was, from a Turkish point of view, a masterstroke.

After Gallipoli, von Sanders was given command in Palestine and Sinai, where he was defeated by General Allenby and the desert forces of Lawrence of Arabia. He was arrested after the war and charged with war crimes, but freed after six months of enquiries. It is sobering to think that, had he been born a generation later, he would have had no chance of becoming a German officer: although the 'von' in his name indicates nobility, his nobleman father was Jewish.

# Brigadier-General William Sitwell
# (1860–1932)

Even judged against the dismal performance of the majority of his fellow generals, Brigadier-General Sitwell ranks among Gallipoli's under-achievers. Less than forty-eight hours after setting foot on the beaches of Suvla he was sacked and ordered home. In command of the 34th Brigade and established on a prominence known as Hill 10, he not only ignored orders to attack from that strong position, but became so confused that he managed to lose control of his troops. The commander who sacked him, Major-General Sir Frederick Hammersley, was partly to blame for the failure because he issued contradictory orders. This, however, does not explain the excessive caution that overcame an officer who had trained at Sandhurst, fought in a string of colonial wars and at one stage commanded mobile columns against the Boers. Like others who lost their reputations on the peninsula he did not know how many Turks he was up against and did not concern himself to find out.

# Winston Churchill (1874–1965)

The Dardanelles Commission, set up to report on a campaign that cost too many lives and ended in failure, came up with the verdict that Winston Churchill was neither solely nor even principally responsible. The verdict of history, less forgiving, has been that Gallipoli was not his finest hour. His initial advice to War Minister Lord Kitchener had been that the Dardanelles could be forced only by a combined operation of ships and troops. When he was bluntly informed that no troops were available, he swung round to the opinion that ships could force a way through on their own. Despite the disastrous failure of the naval attack and despite the string of frustrations that followed on land, Churchill remained vigorously optimistic about the entire enterprise.

By the time the decision was taken to abandon the Gallipoli campaign, Churchill was widely regarded as being an over-enthusiastic amateur strategist, and he had no option but to resign. Always ready to face danger, he applied to be sent to the trenches of France, where he showed courage under fire as commander of an infantry battalion of the Royal Scots Fusiliers. In July 1917, following a political crisis in Westminster that saw Asquith ousted as Prime Minister, the new Premier, Lloyd George, admired Churchill enough to invite him to return to the government as Minister of Munitions. In the next two decades Churchill held a number of important posts, including that of Chancellor of the Exchequer, but Gallipoli remained a stain on his reputation. During spells when he was out of office he turned his overflowing energies into painting, writing, even bricklaying. In the 1930s, he was one of the first politicians, and certainly the most prominent, to warn against the growing menace of Hitler and the Nazi Party.

His warnings were ignored by a government convinced that peace could be preserved by giving in to Hitler's demands. Neville Chamberlain's policy of appeasement failed and a second war against Germany broke out on 3 September 1939. The tide of warfare soon began to run so strongly against Britain that on 10 May 1940, Chamberlain was replaced by Churchill. 'I felt', wrote the new Prime Minister, 'that all my past life had been a preparation for this hour and this trial'. His leadership, and especially his speeches, led the nation to victory after six years of hardship, triumph and sac-rifice. He summed up those days of peril in truly Churchillian style: 'It was the nation and the race dwelling all round the globe that had the lion's heart. I had the luck to be called upon to give the roar.'

When the old warrior was carried down the Thames towards his final resting place the dockside cranes, one by one, dipped their heads in tribute. Any mistakes he may have made over Gallipoli were long forgotten and long forgiven.

# GLOSSARY

**adjutant** an officer who acts as an administrative assistant to a superior officer

**artillery** large guns used in fighting on land

**Base details** a group of soldiers assigned a special duty at the centre of operations

**battalion** a military unit comprised of three or more companies or formations of similar size

**battalion staff officers** officers of a battalion

**battery** a small tactical unit of artillery, usually consisting of two or more troops, each of two, three or four guns

**bogies** (pl.) things that worry or annoy

**brass-hats** (slang) high-ranking officers

**brigade** a large group of soldiers that forms a unit of an army

**brigade major** the principal staff officer to the brigadier in command at the headquarters of a brigade

**Cadet Corps** a group of school pupils receiving elementary military training in a school corps

**calibre** military term referring to the internal diameter of a gun barrel or the diameter of a shell or bullet; ability, distinction

**captain** an officer of the army who holds a rank junior to a major but senior to a lieutenant

**CB** (slang) 'confined to barracks', usually imposed as a punishment

**chlorodyne** a drug containing laudanum and chloroform, with sedative, narcotic and pain-relieving properties

**civvies, in ...** military slang for civilian clothing; not wearing army uniform (see also **civvy**)

**civvy** (slang) a civilian, someone who is not a soldier or combatant

**cold feet** loss or lack of courage or confidence

**Command Staff** officers who advise a military leader and help plan a military operation

**company** a unit of around one hundred troops usually comprising two or more platoons

**Constantinople** the name given to Istanbul from AD 323 to 1923

**corporal** a non-commissioned officer junior to a sergeant in the army

**corps** a large unit of an army, consisting of two or more divisions

**CRE** Commander Royal Engineers

**crocked** (slang) injured

**cushy** (slang) easy, soft, comfortable, undemanding; a 'cushy wound' is a wound that means that a the soldier has to retire from the front line, but which will not leave him permanently injured

**depot** (military) a store for supplies; also, a training and holding centre for recruits and replacements

**division** (military) a major formation, larger than a regiment or brigade but smaller than a corps

**DR** despatch rider (pl. **DRS**)

**dug-out, a** (slang) an officer who has been 'dug out' of retirement and recalled to active duty, usually much to the grievance of those under him

**enfilading** (military) a position or formation subject to fire from a flank

**Expeditionary Force** a group of soldiers sent to fight in a foreign country

**front fire-trench** the military units or elements in a battle that have advanced nearest to enemy lines

**funk** (slang) a coward (noun); to flinch from responsibility through fear (verb)

**funked it up** (slang) a state of nervousness, fear or depression (esp. in the phrase 'in a funk')

**general** an officer of a rank senior to a lieutenant-general, esp. one who commands a large military formation

**harum-scarum** (slang) reckless, impetuous (adj.); in a reckless way or of a reckless nature (adv.); a person who is impetuous or rash nature (noun)

**helio** (slang) see **heliograph**

**heliograph** an instrument with mirrors and a shutter used for sending messages in Morse code by reflecting the sun's rays

**howitzers** a cannon having a short or medium barrel with a low muzzle velocity and a steep angle of fire

**HQRS** (slang) headquarters

**in the air** in the process of being decided; unsettled

**iron rations** emergency food supplies, esp. for military personnel in action

**Jocky** (slang) Scottish, esp. a soldier from the Scottish Highlands

**King's Regulations** (military) the code of conduct for members of the armed forces that deals with discipline, aspects of military law etc.

*kismet* a Turkish word meaning 'fate'

**KR** (see **King's Regulations**)

**lieutenant (Lt)** a military officer holding commissioned rank immediately junior to a captain in the British army

**lieutenant-colonel** military title in British army indicating an officer holding commissioned rank immediately junior to a colonel

**lighter** a flat-bottomed barge used for transporting cargo, especially in loading or unloading a larger ship

**lineman** a man in the squad laying the telephone cable

**major** an officer immediately junior to a lieutenant-colonel in the British army

**MC** Military Cross

**midshipman** a probationary rank held by young naval officers under training, or an officer holding such a rank

**MO** medical officer

**monitor** (formerly) a small heavily armoured shallow-draught warship used for coastal assault

**MSS** manuscript

**neurasthenia** an obsolete medical term for a neurosis characterized by extreme lassitude and inability to cope with any but the most trivial tasks

**neurasthenic** displaying the symptoms of suffering from **neurasthenia**

**NCO** non-commissioned officer

**OC** (slang) Officer Commanding, i.e. officer in charge

**on draft** detachment of military personnel from one unit to another

**Operation Orders** a military or naval action, such as a campaign or manoeuvre, etc

**PBI** (slang) poor bloody infantry

**Piccadilly boy** a phrase, no longer fashionable, that refers to a social climber trying to pass himself off as a 'toff'

**platoon** subdivision of a company, usually divided into three sections of ten or twelve men led by a lieutenant or sub-lieutenant

**PT** physical training or exercise to keep fit

**puttees** a strip of cloth worn wound around the legs from the ankle to the knee, esp. as part of a military uniform in World War I

**QM** quarter master; an officer responsible for accommodation, food and equipment in a military unit

**QMS** (pl.) see **QM**

**queer** differing from the normal or usual in a way regarded as odd or strange

**RAMC** Royal Army Medical Corps

**remounts** place where a fresh horse is acquired esp. (formerly) to replace one killed or injured

**RE section** Royal Engineers section

**rough riding** riding wild or unbroken horses

**routed them out** forced or fetched from a hiding place

**sapper** (slang) a private of the Royal Engineers

**skrimshanking** (slang) to shirk work

**squad** the smallest military formation, typically comprising a dozen soldiers, used especially as a drill formation

**Staff, the** body of officers assisting an officer in high command

**subaltern** a commissioned officer below the rank of captain

**supernumerary mess** an extra (mess) where service personnel eat or take recreation

**Turk** (slang, used in a pejorative sense) a Turkish combatant

**windy** (slang) afraid, frightened, nervous

# BIBLIOGRAPHY

Aspinal-Oglander, Brigadier-General C.F. (compiler),*The History of the Great War Based on the Official Documents of the Committee of Imperial Defence*, Vol. I 'Gallipoli', William Heinemann Ltd., London, 1929.

Barnett, C., *The Great War*, Penguin Books, London, 2003.

Carlyon, L.A., *Gallipoli,* Bantam Books, London, 2003.

Cassar, G.H., *Kitchener's War,* Brassey's Inc., Washington DC, 2004.

De Groot, G.J., *The First World War,* Palgrave Macmillan, Basingstoke, 2001.

Erikson, E.J., *Gallipoli: The Ottoman Campaign*, Pen & Sword, Barnsley, 2010.

Furtado, P. (ed.), *World War I*, Chancellor Press, London, 1993.

Grant, R.G., *World War I: The Definitive Visual Guide*, Dorling Kindersley, London, 2014.

Halpern, P.G., *A Naval History of World War I*, UCL Press, London, 1995.

Keegan, J., *The First World War*, Hutchinson, London, 1999.

Laffin, J., *British Butchers and Bunglers of World War I*, Sutton Publishing, Stroud, 1988.

Mallison, A., *1914 Fight the Good Fight,* Bantam Press, London, 2013.

Mathew, C.C., and B. Harrison (eds.), *The Oxford Dictionary of National Biography*, Oxford University Press in association with The British Academy, Oxford, 2004.

Messenger, C., *Call-to-Arms, The British Army 1914–1918*, Weidenfeld and Nicolson, London, London 2005.

Parker, P., *The Old Lie*, Hambledon Continuum, London, 2007.

Prior, R., *The End of the Myth*, Yale University Press, New Haven, CT, 2009.

Reynolds, D., *The Long Shadow*, Simon and Schuster, London, 2013.

Stevenson, D., *Cataclysm: The First World War as Political Tragedy*, Basic Books, New York, NY, 2005.

Stevenson, D., *1914–1918*, Allen Lane (Penguin Books), London, 2004.

Strachan, H., *The First World* War: To Arms, Oxford University Press, Oxford, 2001.

Taylor, A.J.P., *English History 1914–1945*, Clarendon Press, Oxford, 1965.